Beyond Theatre

a playback theatre memoir

Beyond Theatre

a playback theatre memoir

Jonathan Fox

Tusitala Publishing

Beyond Theatre,
a playback theatre memoir

Copyright © 2015 Jonathan Fox

Tusitala Publishing
137 Hasbrouck Road
New Paltz, NY 12561
USA

www.tusitalapublishing.com

Cover and book design: Carol Hanisch, Word/Graphics.
Front cover photo: The author at Ryoan-ji Temple, Kyoto, Japan.
Back cover photo: Elise Gold.

ISBN 978-0-9889857-5-9

Printed in the United States of America.
5 4 3 2 1

For Jo, Hannah, and Maddy

Contents

Foreword

Playback theatre is linked to the oral tradition, but I found that as I grew older I wanted to tell the story of how we started in a way that was not forever shifting with each retelling in each generation. I wanted to write my version down.

Nothing is more valuable in writing a memoir than notes about events, and all my life I have been a note-taker. But they have been of a very idiosyncratic sort. Some examples:

1/19 Laughter emotions exercise — Bruce says he has "voices" that get in his way

7/5 Good for awareness not to huddle

7/26 Boom stands

1/10 Use socks one or two

(No date): This is a theatre of great versatility. It can play every night for a different group and portray moving, powerful dramas that are different each night

(No date): old tree; sad, torn teenager

My life and work partner Jo Salas used to tease me about the ego it takes to be jotting down thoughts such as these at all hours of the day. I persisted undaunted. But when the time came to use my notes, I found most of them too unfocused to be useful. Even those that have a date lack the year, and by now I am hard-pressed to pinpoint most of them in time. Clearly it was not for this memoir that I did all that scribbling.

Despite this, I have nevertheless made every effort to be accurate.

This is a personal account of what has been important for me about my vocation. It is not a history. There are many events and important people left unmentioned, or scarcely mentioned. This does not mean that I do not value them and their contributions.

It is also not about Jo, my co-founder; and I have tried to protect her privacy while acknowledging her contribution.

I've chosen to end the chronology of this account with my retirement as executive director of the Centre for Playback Theatre in 2010, but the Centre itself did not close its doors. To the contrary, five years later it is thriving (see playbackcentre.org), and I continue to teach for it.

Special thanks to Jo for her reading and critique; to Karen Pittelman, Judy Swallow, and Sarah Urech; and to certain people mentioned in the text to whom I sent snippets in order to check my memory against theirs — you know who you are.

CHAPTER ONE

Upbringing

By any measure I was a lucky fellow. As a young man I had a captivating idea for a kind of theatre that sustained my professional life as well as changed the lives of many others. To explain I have sometimes evoked the river metaphor: I say I was merely the first one to jump into this marvelous current that has carried us all along. But at other times, in silence and not so sanguine, I have pictured myself as a kind of shaggy-haired Sisyphus, dragging a laden cart up an inclined street. It is an old cart with wooden wheels, the cobblestoned surface uneven, and my destination still a long way ahead.

Actually, more than anything else, it has been a journey of searching and discovery (in fact I was not such a young man when the idea came to me), right up to the present, as I set out to write this memoir. Let me start with a train ride from New York City out to central Long Island. Two boys sit together. The older one, no more than eight, holds the other's hand solicitously. The boys are going from their mother's to their father's house, as they do bi-weekly. It is a two-hour ride. The older one—me—fixedly avoids the stares of other passengers, who wonder why two such young children are traveling alone. "You are responsible," says my mother. I am proud, but don't always enjoy it, especially as my little brother, Matthew, needs special attention because of a heart problem. I still remember those journeys. In those years I was constantly in transit toward a different world, negotiating my two homes, the city and the suburb, articulateness and silence, high culture and middle-class culture, absence of affection and nurturance.

My mother had married again. So I had two fathers. They were very different, but both had a similar hope for me: I should become a cosmopolitan professional, most likely a lawyer, a person solidly within the circle of influence and accomplishment.

It is a year or two later. This time with my new stepbrother, Peter. We are answering the door at our parents' annual New Year's Day party. We wear matching blazers and ties. When the door rings, we answer. I notice the expensive shoes, the polished faces. One of us takes a luxurious overcoat, while the other guides the arrivals to the parlor. Later we might, under my stepfather's supervisory eye, take a group of guests on a tour of the paintings (mostly American modern). This house was one of the many elegant settings of my youth, along with the carpeted parlors of my boarding school and the majestic museums and theatres of New York City.

One day at my father's I came across a suitcase in the attic. Inside were programs and clippings from his years as a professional actor. A secret cache! As I read, heart pounding, I saw he had done well in this theatre world. I found myself angry as well as excited. He knew that from the time I started school I loved being in plays. Why didn't he tell me about his own life in the theatre? Why didn't he encourage me?

Over the years he would occasionally relate a tidbit. The night he passed out from drinking. He spent most of his time during the production as a messenger boy between the director and her lover. What emerged was a dissolute life and his sense that it had been wasteful. He never mentioned art, or poetry, or ensemble, or the audience.

My stepfather did not like children. So we were sent away— to school in the winter, to camp in the summer. One camp was very small and run by a Quaker couple. I remember walking along wooded tracks with Leon, the director. He did not say much, but it was comfortable walking beside him. On early summer mornings, we looked for birds together. He directed my gaze to the yellow warbler and the indigo bunting—so graceful, so colorful, so musical, so vulnerable. He did not need many words to get his points across. To spot them and enjoy them you had to really look and listen; you had to make yourself still and small.

My stepfather did not want me to be small. "Whatever you do, be number one," he would say. He himself was an ambitious, even rapacious man, giving his advice from the pinnacle of his success (but before his subsequent fall). My father was more reserved. "Be a carpenter, if you want," he would say, masking his true hopes.

My father's failure to encourage me, to praise me, to hold up the flag for me, to trumpet his love for me may have had its roots in a deep reluctance to make any kind of over proud statement that future events might prove untrue. This was, I believe, his cultural legacy as a Jew. It was also, perhaps, born out of a conviction that our deepest truths are not to be named, but held in the treasure chest of the heart.

He did love. I always knew that. I don't know how. Was it the expression on his face when he first saw me after a two-week absence? Was it how it felt inside his hug? Was it his coming to sit beside me on my heavy Sunday evenings when I knew I would soon have to return to the city?

My stepfather's was an intellectual house. When we were bad, we had to memorize poems. Returning from a concert or play, we were expected to give an oral report. It was a kind of schooling. Be number one. Be articulate.

Once when I am about ten or eleven at Leon's camp we are taken to an outdoor concert. Sitting on a hillside in upstate New York, surrounded by long grass ringed with ash and oak trees as the languid evening settled into dusk, I feel at one with the world and everything in it. The orchestra, situated at the edge of a pristine lake, plays from below. The music soars into the evening air. A light shines within as well as without. Musicians and audience are held in the embrace of a benign earth. The moment is short, but its memory of feeling the oneness of all things holds fast.

We are at boarding school. I am a freshman trying out for the track team, sprinting against the other boys. One runner is my stepbrother, Peter. I edge ahead and finish first. A triumph, beating the upperclassmen. Why doesn't it feel better?

When I look at my older brother, I am uneasy, now that I have beaten him. When I look at my little brother, I have such complex feelings, since I am so healthy. Everything comes easy to me, a scholar athlete. Why doesn't it feel better?

Sport appealed: the physical part—blood pounding, the body cutting through space, the quick thinking, the doing together.

We had a dog in my mother and stepfather's house, the shaggy kind, very sweet. When they went on a trip, they put her in a kennel. When she grew old, they did not want to be disturbed by infirmity. So they sent her away—to the kennel, never to return.

True to form I became a literary young man, editor of my high-school newspaper, an English major at university. What drew me, however, were not the polished sentences of the Victorians, but the rough verses of Old and Middle English. I liked the early pieces, like the *Second Shepherd's Play*, where humor melds into blessing, and simple gifts—a tennis ball, a cherry, a bird—will satisfy the Lord. I liked the ancient stories, too, the tales that were older than their writers.

At university, they computed the grades to hundredths of a percentage point, and when my adviser, a young turk soon to be renowned, announced at the end that I would miss Harvard high honors by mere hundredths, there was no sympathy in his manner, no regret that he might have helped me over.

I might have found refuge in the oppositional milieu that was bursting into life around me in 1964: a world of psychotropic discovery, sexual freedom, and political action, principally against the war in Vietnam. But the sound of anti-war demonstrations was faint in my ears, and for me, Alpert and Leary were mere names in the newspaper, even though they were on the same campus. Undergraduates I knew were seduced by a hypersexual cohort of junior faculty, but they did not act liberated. My roommate worked for the Kennedys over the summer, but seemed to spend most of the time drinking at parties.

I did apply to study law after graduating, as the fathers had advised, but that path held no appeal. Should I take up a fellowship to study in New Zealand? It lay so refreshingly far away—from the speaking smart, the getting ahead, the avenues of elegance, the being on top.

Clown Car

New Zealand has a land mass roughly the size of Colorado, but a population less than the cities of Manchester, Santiago, or Montreal. In other words, there's lots of bush surrounded by lots of water and relatively few people. From almost every vantage point is the sight of the sea, the dustless sky, steep hills. I was amazed how hardy people were. They did not worry about dunes so big they felt like deserts. Or about dangerous water, or sheep at the end of the road, or the mountains across the bay that did not seem to have a name. They did not seem to feel the damp chill inside their unheated houses. New Zealand had a benign climate; a land of life-sustaining rain, unless you are riding your horse down a hill in it; a land of fresh breezes, unless you're out on the water in your sailboat when a storm blows in; a land of bright sun, unless you are trekking without a hat.

I toured its exposed pathways with mouth agape, coming as I did from such a large urban conglomeration in the world, where walls of concrete, brick, and steel limited my vision and I never noticed the phases of the moon.

I arrived with a trunk that included three pairs of flannel trousers, forty-one button-down dress shirts, and a fistful of ties. They didn't fit the landscape.

Life in this azure and verdant country, so bare of bus fumes and bustle, seemed only half real. I bought an eighteen year-old car with a ten horsepower engine. Pasting a sign on the side that said "Jaguar," I invite girls to ride in my "Jag." It was fun to be silly, so far away from the things that weighed me down.

New Zealand in 1966 was a country looking for its story. Was New Zealand an adjunct of England, or its own dominion (England ran the New Zealand foreign office until well after World War II)? Was it an obedient little brother to the US, or a shaper of its own national policy (it buckled on sending troops to Vietnam, but stood fast in refusing harbor to United States nuclear submarines)?

I was looking for my story, too. Not surprisingly, far from New York's noisy streets and crowds, I felt very much a cosmopolitan. Under little pressure, I read with leisure, including earlier ignored classics: Tolstoy and Joyce, Franz Fanon, Michael Harrington,

Malcolm X, and Eldridge Cleaver; Gutierrez and Illich; Ginsberg and the Beats. I jotted down key phrases. I took notes for future novels.

When a professor invited me to expand a paper I had written into a master's thesis (in political science), I agreed. My dissertation was called "State Aid to the Arts in New Zealand."

It was in New Zealand that I took my first activist baby steps, publicly opposing the US war in Southeast Asia.

Most important, I met someone. We were strongly drawn to each other from the start. Her name was Jo Salas. She was six years younger, but we had lots in common—a love of literature and the arts, a mixed Jewish background, and a sensitivity to bullying, political and otherwise. We spent all our time together, and it was not long before I came to understand that my blasé Down Under life had turned a corner. When it was time for me to go back to America, it broke our hearts. I vowed to return. Jo's loving parents urged me not to make false promises.

The story had gotten serious. On my last day, waiting for the flight to be called with Jo as close to my side as she could get, I did not notice whether it stormed or the sun shone. What registered were the tears wetting our own cheeks.

Down in the Ditch
In order to avoid being drafted to fight in what we called the Vietnamese War, I joined the Peace Corps and was posted to Nepal.

It was an awkward situation from the start. Two men, one a minor government official, the other a servant, were exhorting me not to do what I was doing, which was untying my work boots, bought to walk the dusty tracks of Nepal. The boots cost more than a month's salary in this locale, but they represented a minor gesture in the old (the United States). "Here's some cash; buy a couple of things you will need," our superiors had told us. Some of us bought toilet paper; some bought candy bars; a few of us, work boots. All were useless.

I was being escorted to my assigned village for the first time. We were facing a river, the first of five to ford (there were no bridges). The servant would carry me across the river, my new co-worker insisted. It was normal, he said. Even though I didn't understand his words very well, I knew, as I bent down to undo the laces, that I had not come to Nepal to be carried on someone's back.

They had told us never to walk barefoot because we would be exposed to parasites. But those experts did not themselves know about the numerous rivers without bridges or ferries and a rainy season where thick mud lay at every turn. If one wore footwear at all, it needed to be of the easy on, easy off variety. We did what the locals did. We wore flip-flops. We took them off when needed. And we got worms.

So the work boots gathered dust in my suitcase—until it came time to leave that village two years later, when I faced another problem. However impractical as footwear, the boots would be prized as a trophy. Lugging them out was folly, but leaving them behind brought with it the difficult diplomatic problem of whom to give (or sell) them to.

It seemed there was no good solution for those damned boots.

In Nepal I learned to live in the manner of billions of the world's inhabitants: without running water or electricity. On two meals a day, always the same, eaten with the hand. In a mud hut. For furniture, my hut had two rope cots, one for inside, one for outside. It had an earthen floor, which belonged to the rats as much as to me.

You could ride a bicycle if you had to go somewhere, but most of the time, you walked, due to mud or excessive rutting. I walked through jungle, with packs of lemurs glaring at me. I walked through rice paddies. I walked through rivers.

If living in New Zealand had been a door opener to nature, Nepal was the initiation, the ordeal. A further stripping away. At university I had studied orality; here I lived it. Most could not read and write. But they could talk. They could do what V.S. Naipaul calls "play-talk." They knew where you had been and what you had done, and they could embellish the tale to their own ends, using a language tailor-made for telling stories. Occasionally wandering bards appeared to sing their tales, but the villagers largely ignored them. To follow their verses was too difficult, and so I ignored them, too. What did interest me were the festival dances. A man always dressed as a woman. These dances were full of mischief. In the closeness of the setting, with villagers tightly surrounding the performers, a dancer's glance at one or another onlooker was all it took to convey a saucy hidden meaning.

There was a drama to the natural life. The drivers struggling to get their oxen to pull, looking like beasts themselves. The cobra flaring at you. The sun setting behind the pipal tree. Sitting about a fire in the dry season as the day cooled and stars popped out. The day I fell into the irrigation ditch on my way into town, the news arrived before me. When you walked the narrow path through muddy fields and someone approached from the other direction, you had lots of time to think about your moment of meeting, where one person would have to step aside.

My closest neighbors were the schoolteacher and his wife. They had one son. I yearned to play with him. But he was too terri- fied to come near. "I'll tie you up and leave you with the American. He eats little boys!" said his father repeatedly to make him behave. It was hopeless. This teacher did not believe in a spherical earth. He was an adult who could not do sums. With his false pride, his ignorance, his callow cruelty, and his short stature, he struck me as a kind of troll, a gnome, an imp. My one-world romanticism dropped away. Between the first and the third world there was more than a material gulf. There was a chasm of education and knowledge.

Ignorance flourished on both sides. The US government had enlisted me to show Nepali farmers how to use modern agricul- tural methods. My job was actually to persuade farmers to take loans to buy fertilizer and better seed. Only the goods never ar- rived. That was enough to eliminate my daily work. But there was a bigger problem. What did I, the New York literary man, know of rice cultivation? My years in Nepal provided me, the scion of a rich country, with a special kind of post-graduate education, but whether it offered anything to the Nepalis was highly questionable.

One day I returned to my hut to see an old lady crouching on the verandah. When I went inside to sleep, she was still there. When I awoke the next day, she was still there. When she spoke, I could not understand her. She did not seem to understand me. I asked the villagers about her, and they said she was a female sadhu, a sadhvi, a holy beggar. She has to go, I said. She should not be expelled, they replied. I was very put out. In this place of no privacy, even my tiny verandah was no more my own. Whenever I sat on my cot, she was there, crouching in the corner. If she saw me eat something, she asked for some. If she saw me use something, she wanted one. The sadhvi remained for one week, then another. I felt desperate. Toward the end of the second week, there was a moment when I looked over at her. She looked me in the eye, smiled, and made a gesture imitating me perfectly. I laughed spontaneously, suddenly fully aware of her intelligence, her presence, her personhood. My heart opened to her. The next day she was gone.

Jo and I married at the tail end of 1969. For a while we lived in a remote part of England, where our daughter Hannah was born. I wrote short stories. But unlike the epic tales of heroes and turns of fortune I studied at university, what came out of me were dull slices of life with constricted, angst-ridden protagonists. After a year or so, I had to admit defeat. I couldn't find the *story* in my stories. I started to write plays and radio scripts. This was a bit better. Inspired by the writing of the composer John Cage, I wrote dramatic pieces that incorporated chance elements; I composed poems called "cut-ups" using the I Ching.

We returned to the United States and settled in New London, a small coastal city in Connecticut. It was 1972, still a period of national upheaval: the American president authorized continued fierce bombing of Vietnam as well as ordering illegal acts at home (Watergate). I had been away for over five years. I was no booster of the status quo. I had not been seduced by my stepfather's call to be "number one" and pursue the power and prestige of mainstream accomplishment; why would I be a patriotic follower of a strong-arming, hubristic nation? However, fiction writing, my childhood ambition, had reached a dead end. Although I hardly admitted it to myself, by now I had no clear prospects. I still loved stories. But what would I do to sustain my family and find my satisfaction?

Chapter Two

Calling

"The notice said, "Everyday Acting." I signed up because I had always liked the idea of being in a play, but was too shy to try out. The class took place in the children's room of the public library. We sat on those little chairs! The teacher, a man with very long curly hair, surprised me right away. "We are not going to do a play," he said. "We're going to make one up." I had no idea what he was talking about. Then he asked us all to stand up and wiggle our shoulders. It was pretty stupid. Eventually he said it was time to make the story. We could all make suggestions. I really had no good ideas, but when it came time to pick the roles—we could do that, too—it just came out of my mouth. "I'll be the gangster," I said. It didn't take us long to act out the story—about a guy and a girl walking home from a date and being asked the time by a gangster who had hostages in his black Cadillac. It was over before I knew it. I talked tough as the gangster—or tried to. And moved my shoulders back and forth like I've seen tough guys do. It was fun. I don't know if I'll go back next week. Those little chairs!"

So goes the imaginary report from a man in my first class. My method was very low key. It was theatre at its crudest. There was no focus on stage presence, no audience. There was nothing particularly stimulating for the mind or challenging for the body. In fact I had trouble knowing what to call it. What characterized this approach, if anything, was the enactment of a group "story." The participants could play the character they wanted. I did not know their life stories, but as I gently directed our playmaking, I sensed the biographical echoes and made suggestions that I felt might in some vague way energize individual actors.

The first professional request came from four couples, who asked my help in preparing a piece for their guru. No sooner had I said my "Let's stand up and wiggle," than they started to talk energetically, even argumentatively, among each other, and in fact, my facilitation was over. Apparently, three minutes of warm-up had unleashed all their conflicts. Needless to say, there was no play for the guru that season.

But after each of these forays, no matter how unsuccessful, I was not discouraged, for I had discovered something in myself and was overjoyed simply to be in touch with it. What especially pleased me was the chance to facilitate naive participants to feel creative; to make up stories on the spot; to throw plans out the window in order to follow the adventurous path of a group's mutual exploration.

In hindsight one might label these workshops more than anything else a creative dramatics workshop for adults. Or a very basic form of community-based theatre.[1] Or a rudimentary form of drama therapy. I called it simply "personal improvisation."

Then parents from an alternative elementary school approached me to help them write a play to perform for their kids. I applauded their idea, but suggested that instead of my writing a play for them, together we would develop one. First I worked with them on freeing up creativity and expressiveness. Then we developed a story based on characters just one step away from the personality of the actors, producing a finished product that was high on authenticity if rough as art.

After the play was over, the parent/actors did not want to stop, and a theatre company was born. We called ourselves "It's All Grace." With her classical training in violin and beautiful voice, it was no surprise that Jo became the musician. My notes written at the time assert that It's All Grace "values the welfare of the group above its projects and performances." At the same time, "performance is the razor's edge of our endeavor." If there was a contradiction here, it showed in our work, which involved many very intense rehearsals over a two-year period and only two performances.

I had not liked our domineering dramatics coach, but that was not the only reason I had stopped doing theatre in high school: I didn't appreciate the seemingly endless repetitions of the same lines and actions, or the hierarchy in the drama club.

Looking back, however, I had always felt a strong pull to acting and had participated in many school plays. I liked being in a charged relationship with the audience. I liked the feel of a projected voice in my chest. I liked the movement, the timing, and the teamwork. I liked the camaraderie. And being a growing boy I even enjoyed sometimes getting to kiss the girl.

Then there was the knowledge that my father had once been an actor in a famous repertory company in New York.

Thus leading my new Everyday Acting workshops and directing the It's All Grace company was a kind of return. I started to read with passionate interest books about creative dramatics (Way, Slade, Heathcote), modern dance (Humphries, Graham), and especially experimental theatre (Artaud, Grotowski, Schechner, Chaikin, Gregory, Brook).

I pored over articles in the Drama Review, reading excitedly about a company in Holland (Werkteater) that did not confine its performances to theatres; about Topeng dance drama in Bali; about Kabuki and Noh theatre. I felt like I was reading in a delicious language I had never known I knew.

Within a period of months:

I joined a dance class and found a mime teacher. I did not care that at thirty I was too old to be starting this kind of study.

I began to show up at the nearby National Theatre of the Deaf, eventually being invited to assist Marjorie Sigley on a project for deaf actors. She was a British T.I.E. (Theatre in Education) director who ran a children's theatre company in New York. (Later I was to work briefly as an actor in her Young People's Theatre.)

I absorbed the Grotowski process when Jerry Rojo, a protégé of Richard Schechner and a theatre professor at the University of Connecticut, hired me to be a writer for a Grotowski-inspired production.

I developed an informal relationship with the locally based American Dance Festival, which expanded to include performances and workshops from a group of seven NYC-based experimental theatres. They were funded for "community outreach" and sometimes turned to me to help them organize the events. In this way I observed up close the work of Andre Gregory, Lee Breuer, Richard Schechner, Meredith Monk, and others.

During this period I also saw Zerka Moreno direct an open session psychodrama and was struck by the intimacy and the intensity of the process. I saw it as a powerful form of popular theatre. I was also intrigued by her preamble about J. L. Moreno's Theatre of Spontaneity in Vienna.[2]

Before long I was running various drama projects, such as a series of workshops for youth, and I taught drama briefly at a drug rehabilitation facility. These jobs pleased me because I got paid for them, but I knew they were not in themselves what I was looking for.

In a two-year period, my life had changed. Proximity and enthusiasm had enabled me to get a crash course in nontraditional theatre. I was no longer a writer; I was a theatre person. But what kind of theatre person, exactly? Clearly it valued the spirit of children, the well-being of actors, and a spontaneous creative process. But what about performances? And what about the "art?"

Nureyev aloft

We were in a well-appointed Greenwich Village apartment with lots of polished wood and a series of striking photos on the walls of Rudolph Nureyev in motion. I was standing next to the grand piano with my pants unbuttoned. The man at the piano, music director of the children's theatre production I was performing in (Marjorie Sigley had hired me to act in two of her children's theatre pieces at New York's City Center), urged me to relax. It was a private singing lesson. "Try it again," he said. "From here," he added, putting his hand on my lower abdomen. He was a small man with a smoky beard and a paunch. I knew he had hopes about me, and they did not concern singing.

As for me, I was enjoying my brush with the New York actors' life. I had been elated to sign a contract, to take part in the routine of walking daily across the famed City Center stage, to chat in the dressing room. I even enjoyed finding myself in this dusky Village flat for my singing lesson, with its elegant restaurant below, where we would later share good wine and coquilles St. Jacques.

He was doing well, my music director, and I appreciated his attention, but I was never seriously tempted, either by him or the world he came from. After a few months I returned to Connecticut, my family, and my own crude form of theatre, which couldn't have been more different from singing numbers, learning a script, blocking action, donning costumes, and performing in a black box space. Mine was a determinedly poor theatre that did not even seek out a stage. It used a simple kind of dramatic language that while unknown and unrecognized, nevertheless would develop a grammar of its own that would include play, no script, informal theatre, and collaboration.

What I cherished was that fertile state of children absorbed in a game—the voices, the energy, the joining together, the joy. Not so easy to access as an adult, at least for many, but we all have the capacity to drop into childishness, naiveté, laughter, being in touch. It was perhaps paradoxical for me to facilitate such passages, since as a person my way of being in the world was solitary, serious, even burdened. Yet inside me there has always been a clown that can play with kids and make them laugh. The clown's path, when I could find my way there, has been my own via negativa—at odds with the overarching seriousness of the experimental theatre movement, my main frame of reference at that time.

Furthermore, from the start I believed in "never too much." This credo also stood in strong contrast to the Artaudian and Grotowski traditions. I could feel this as I participated in workshops with Andre Gregory, Lee Breuer, or Richard Schechner and Jerry Rojo. Sure, let's get our body working; let's loosen up; let's release some energy, I felt. But let us not exhaust or depress ourselves with enforced rigor. One way to help performers get outside of the confines of everyday thought, so that their mind/body will experience a release, is to dance, I found. Dancing also promotes connection and joy. Another is to engage in nonsense. Thus my warm-ups, even once I found myself directing It's All Grace, were often like child's play because I wanted to encourage my actors to be as playful as very young children.

If we can truly play, it will help us relax. If we taste joy, it will also help us be open to one another and to the audience.

All this doesn't sound like much, and in a way it isn't. It can be half-defined by what it is not: It is anti-systematic. It does not use games to teach specific skills. It does not prize competition. Or go to the bone.

Play. Talk. Listen. Laugh. Find joy. Just enough to get stretched, relaxed, awake, alive, open, ready. Ready for the spontaneous moment, the surprise of the unexpected story, the stepping over the threshold into risk and change, whatever the context—whether performance, workshop, or something in between.

Empty Stage

In connection with play, I sought freedom from set words and actions—i.e., improvisation. There was my father, who had spent months as a playing card in a production of *Alice in Wonderland*, or myself, whose big solo in the Young People's Theatre production was in the song, "Circles Go Round and Round." Can such roles, repeated every day, sustain an intelligent, creative person? The work of Second City in Chicago interested me. It was at least improvised. But its comic/satiric emphasis at the expense of a full range of emotional content dimmed its allure. Inspired in part by Viola Spolin and theatre games, it tended to avoid the serious. This was also true about Theatre Sports, a competitive improvisation format that achieved significant popularity later. The companies working in the experimental theatre most assuredly did not avoid the serious, and they used improvisation to develop their pieces, but then set them, usually including a script. I did not want scripts.

As the years passed, Forum Theatre and the work of Augusto Boal became a widespread form of interactive theatre with unscripted outcomes, but the provocation was always set. Boal's theatre started with set scenarios.

I have attended opera at La Scala in Milan, the ballet at the Bolshoi in Moscow, Molière at the Comédie-Française in Paris, Shakespeare at the Globe Theatre in London, and savored many fine productions on Broadway. But what excited me most was the call of an empty stage, the chance to start from zero.[3] I wanted us to walk onto the playing space truly without a plan, a game, or a script. To be given a narrative, then to confront the challenge of how to render it on stage with shape, color, sounds and movement, meaning; and on top of it all, to do it with an audience watching and waiting to see what you will come up with—this extreme challenge excited me tremendously. It's All Grace satisfied some of these yearnings, but left others unfulfilled. I found myself continuing to stare at the horizon.

Orange Sky

It is fifteen years into the future. I am standing on a balcony looking out over a southern European city, wine glass in hand, chatting with a friend from what I would call the "theatre theatre." The air is mild. The sky is orange with the end of day. Sounds of life rise up from the streets below.

"Improvisation is so enlivening," he says. In a flash I know that he is about to say something critical. "But you have to admit yourself that the quality of performance, the standard, is often very low."

He has a point. The standard is frequently low.

"I mean," he goes on, "do you not sometimes feel a bit abashed at what you have wrought?"

He is trying to provoke me.

"You are forgetting that improvisation is context-sensitive," I say. "Often it is performed in intimate circumstances. If the performers' skill level is not at a level that would satisfy you, it doesn't need to be. They are able to satisfy their audiences. Hopefully they will always strive to improve. In fact I believe they do improve."

"But we are men of the theatre. We want to see actors thrilling us on stage with their language and their emotion. We want to see color and movement and music."

"Of course. I am interested in these things, too. But also in more than these things."

"Have some more wine," he says, reaching toward my glass.

As I drink, I reflect.

I have been dealing with these issues for a long time, first intellectually, weighing the respective merits of participation and excellence in my New Zealand master's thesis, then practically with It's All Grace. One issue is cultural. The Western theatre has its traditions, one of which is a certain concept of rehearsal, basically consisting of a period of intensive preparation for as long as time and money allow. But it was not always this way. Peter Brook famously describes Shakespeare's theatre as "rough and holy"; we now know that while actors at the Globe carefully learned lines, they typically actually rehearsed for only a day prior to debuting a piece. Thus the plays were performed with an edge of uncertainty and very little in the way of polish.[4] I wish I had been alive then, for I was drawn more to homespun performance than the flawless speeches and mesmerizing routines of professional performers.

As an adult I saw the festival dances in Nepal and the Morris dancers in England, villagers performing for their neighbors. I had treasured reading about the Medieval so-called "miracle plays," simple productions enacted on movable carts. In my thirties I had an eye-opening experience in Norway. It was the end of a month-long training, and when it came time to plan for the last-night party, they appointed a committee to produce an entertainment. I remember my skepticism that something successful could be organized by a casually chosen committee just two days beforehand (despite my proclivities, I assumed trained talent would have to be involved!). But the result was stunning. There were skits and dances. There was a little orchestra. There were poetry and singing. My heart-thumping realization afterward was that anyone there could have served on the committee and created an entertaining evening because, as Norwegians, all drew on a centuries-old native dramatic tradition learned at family and community gatherings.

Being American, on the other hand, from a pioneering country with a thin, heterogeneous culture, I had no such tradition to draw on. To be sure, there was precious little of this kind of informal dramatic activity in the mid-century America I grew up in. But did absence of background mean we could not use innate faculties to create deep and hilarious moments on the stage?

During our training for going to Nepal I had directed a skit which hinted at this future interest—a humorous version of the

Pocahontas-John Smith story created for our Thanksgiving dinner celebration. What stands out in memory was my equal interest in the well-being of participants and the artistic outcome. For example, I persuaded one of the Nepali language teachers, a fellow flown from rural Nepal straight to California and plunked into class as a language teacher, to play Pocahontas, and a shy American to play Captain Smith. It was a process not without risk. Would they be able to bring off the roles? When the audience laughed, would they be pleased rather than offended? When the event seemed to succeed on both personal and dramatic fronts, I was gratified. This was a very homespun approach. We did not rehearse a musical. We did not learn a text. It was not unlike the play within a play in *A Midsummer Night's Dream*, except as featured performers, instead of Bottom and Peter, we had Sharmagi and Ken, my language teacher and my fellow volunteer.

Later the It's All Grace theatre company, like the Mummer and Miracle players, would perform mainly outdoors with simple equipment. Our work was also a form of poor theatre and often seemed just one step beyond the spontaneous enactments of young children or the adults playing charades.

Are such dramatizations unworthy of serious attention because they use untrained talent and have minimum rehearsal? Not to me. Is a performance to be dismissed because the actors rehearsed one evening a week, or less? Not to me. It is a question of emphasis, or perhaps taste. So often in the theatre theatre to reach for the highest standard at a cost of millions produces only mediocrity, while not infrequently citizen actors in the informal theatre can stop your heart. Although changes in cultural communication have weakened the grip of the traditional arts, the concept of creativity handed down by an earlier aristocratic culture still prevails. So many will not dare to consider stepping onto the stage because they know they cannot act like Meryl Streep or sing like Pavarotti. I believe we can make a choice to put our attention to "c," ordinary creativity, as well as "C," elite creativity. We can accept the accordion as well as the flute, rap as well as *bel canto*, the street or gymnasium as a practice space as well as the professional studio.[5]

I know my wine-drinking friend will not accept this idea of

the informal theatre. His concept of quality demands intensive rehearsal periods. In the end, as we lean over the balcony looking out at the darkening city, I feel that he does not want to argue questions residing at the core of the Western theatre tradition. He is simply asserting his allegiance to craft and art.

"You have a point," I say. "Let's toast the theatre!"

"To theatre!" he replies, as we clink glasses and drink.

Tambourine

There was a telling moment in the summer of 1974 when the It's All Grace theatre company went to a performance of Schechner's Performance Group. It was an intimate space, with the audience on bleachers. Musical instruments were hung from the stands for the actors to use in the production. One of my It's All Grace actors sensed that the tambourine hanging next to her seat sent an ambiguous message — on the one hand, it said, "There is no separation between performer and audience, since we can leave our props among you"; but on the other hand, it was only to be used by the actors at their chosen moment in the play. So Alexandra decided to expose the hypocrisy. She picked up the tambourine and began to play it. The play stopped. An actor came out of role and asked her to stop. Then they resumed. Alexandra hit it again, and again, until they ejected her from the hall.

Like many experimental groups of the period, the Performance Group paid lip service to the idea of no separation between actors and audience. Their director called for a "village" atmosphere, but in fact mounted scripted productions where the audience was not to depart from its traditional confines. This was in fact a far cry from the village atmosphere I had known in Nepal, where performers were villagers themselves and little children stepped into the performers' circle.

The workshops I offered did not emphasize performance, set routines, or text, and what emerged depended on the collaboration of the participants. The It's All Grace performance, while roughly set, invited audience participation. My approach was opposite to what we experienced with the Performance Group. To demarcate the ritual space for theatre was essential — we never sought to rub out this line—but we also wanted genuine collaboration from the onlookers. It was this stark difference that sparked Alexandra's rebellion.

Related to this was an idea of inclusion that slowly took form under the influence of Moreno's psychodrama, the therapeutic form of role playing that I had started to study. His concept of sociometry, focusing on the dynamic of groups, outlined the mechanics of social cohesion. Suddenly my Thanksgiving Peace Corps skit took on new significance. It had been more than simple entertainment. A purpose of the intervention was to integrate Sharmaji and Ken, to build positive connections between them and the others. This idea would take on added meaning in the years to come.

CHAPTER THREE

Discovery

Early in 1974, thirty-one years old, the director of a theatre company that performed so rarely as to be virtually unknown even in our own community, with a young family to support and no regular means of doing it, I wondered what was to become of me. I had a passion for theatre, but a decidedly strange form of it that cherished freedom from scripts, playfulness, and interaction with the audience.

Wandering aimlessly down the main street of New London, Connecticut, one day, a street crowned by a bright sky sloping steeply to the blue waters of a river, I stumbled into a coffee shop and upon the crystallizing idea I sought. In my mind's eye I looked down at a row of actors, as if from above. They were sitting upstage, facing the audience with full attention. The audience, a small group, was in turn regarding at the actors. The light, the ambience, was warm and inviting. Between actors and audience lay a wooden stage. It was not raised. I knew that the actors were part of the same small community as the audience. They were waiting for someone to tell a story, which they would then act out on the spot.

The crux of the idea consisted of the nature of the story. It would be a personal story. Something real, not made up. The audience would be interested because the teller might well be a neighbor and the story about a subject that mattered to them, too.

In my vision there was no offstage. Every moment was always visible, as in Japanese traditional theatre. Despite the intimacy of the space, the domain of the audience was distinct from the stage. An audience member would have to come onto the edge of the stage to become the narrator.

Later the format became more clear. An audience member would come to a position at the edge of the stage to the audience's left to tell her or his story, interviewed by a company member we came to call the conductor. Opposite them, at extreme stage left, again like Japanese theatre, would be a musician.

Pulsing with excitement, I ran home and told Jo, then the It's All Grace theatre company members about the new idea. I wanted us to start experimenting right away. This new direction would be a change for the group, since we had been working on devised pieces. For what was implied in the new vision was playmaking that was completely spontaneous. Like the arts in traditional cultures, such as Aboriginal sand painting or a Native American vision dance, the process of creation could not be separated from the product.

Would it work in a modern, Western context, where audiences were used to the controlled sequences of the theatre theatre? Would anyone in the audience want to tell? Most importantly, what kinds of stories would come? Would the actors understand them? How would the tellers react after watching their story embodied? How would the audience feel about it? Such questions only excited me. In fact the questions were embodied in the idea. They would arise with each performance. This metadrama would carry its own suspense. While the basic idea hearkened back to oral traditional narrative, it did not evoke a specific folk form, and the metadrama introduced a post-modern element.

As I made notes in subsequent days, there was also a popular theatre aspect: "Five to eight folk, in simple but brightly colored clothing. They come on singing, moving, talking, showing themselves in a genuine, unpolished way. Always spontaneous. Getting out their energy. Warming up the audience. Involving them."

Jo liked the new concept and some of the other company members joined in; but others were reluctant. After all, this was not what they signed up for. For our first practical try-out we went to a friend's dance studio that replicated to some extent the warm atmosphere of my vision. We put my idea into action, as best we could. It was very crude. But I remember a story from that night:

I was on my way to a therapy session with a new therapist. I was nervous, and left in lots of time. But on the way, in spite of checking how to get there beforehand, I got lost. I got more and more anxious as I drove around an unsettled rural area looking for the right road. I finally found it, getting there just in time.

In this narrative the teller experiences an ordeal on the way to meeting a wise person empowered with helping her find an answers to a conundrum (the problem of her life). She wanders onto an unknown path, surrounded by trees with no one to ask. It is a classic story—archetypal. She needs to be lost before she can be found. Not coincidentally, although certainly unconsciously, the teller's personal story also paralleled our story of the evening, where all of us present, actors and invited guests, entered the somewhat dangerous-seeming domain of spontaneous personal theatre to see what we would find.

But we didn't need to analyze it to appreciate it as a story rich for dramatic interpretation. I felt that if this new approach could evoke stories like that, it had a future.

After two months, pushed by me, the group attempted a performance, which we titled "an evening of life theatre." It took place in a church basement in August 1974. The result was mixed. One person commented that "the players' energy seemed down." Another said that "it seemed more of a workshop format, better not intended for audiences." Many of the actors were undecided. But if anything, I emerged more committed, aware that the idea would spark opposition in many and that to be sure we had a long way to go to develop it properly.

In time it became clear that It's All Grace as a whole did not have the heart to switch approaches, and Jo and I began to talk of starting a new group. This decision coincided with a plan to move from Connecticut to New York State. So the era of It's All Grace came to an end in order to make space for a new theatre project to begin.

Churchyard Moon

The first meeting of the new company took place in the community room of a church on November 13, 1975 in Beacon, New York. The space was not cozy, but had a nice floor and big windows overlooking a graveyard. I stood before eleven invited participants, Jo included, and stated my plan. We would rehearse five times a month, four weekday evenings and one weekend day. We would have a development phase; we would test out the idea in performance; then, if we liked the results, we would proceed with a longer-term professional program.

"I never want us to do this full-time," I declared, hinting at my idea of a citizen actor, one who lived and worked in the community, while developing special skills for the stage. I also said that I wanted us to perform for many different kinds of groups. Not all of them would have money to pay us. In fact, for every two times we earned money I wanted us to perform one time for free. (How idealistic, how innocent that statement turned out to be!)

I told them to wear the right clothes for physical work; I wanted them all to keep notebooks (again, how idealistic). I also told them that I wanted the theatre to be as good for the actors as it was for the audience and that it was essential for us to tell our own stories.

The actors listened to me with expressions that were hard to fathom. I am sure that many masked their skepticism.

After my speech, we did sound and movement exercises. Then we acted out three of our own personal stories. I made notes about what worked and what didn't. By the end of the four-hour evening, the moon had risen over the graveyard, and with a great sigh of relief, after the months of dreaming, I knew we were under way.

Why did we find ourselves in the Hudson Valley of New York State rather than, say, New York City, arts capital of the United States (perhaps the world), only a short train ride away? A reason of principle was that small-town culture, with its civility and other face-to-face values, seemed more congruent with the idea of a theatre of real stories than that of the Big Apple. Moreover, the scripted theatre, an outgrowth of cities, was a theatre of strangers. Ours was to be a theatre of neighbors and hearken back to communal times. Better establish it outside the urban center. A practical reason was that it was cheaper to get by in the country, where you could rent a place to live for less than half the price in the city and grow food in the backyard as well.

This choice of location for the new company was to have lasting consequences for our future. Whatever positive reasons there were for avoiding the big city, it was also true that outside it there was much less chance for the well-paid performance.

The Plumber and the Nurse

Once having had the idea for a theatre of personal story, it did not take me long to realize that there was a psychological element to it. I had known nothing about psychology, theoretically or practically. Moreover, even though I wanted this new theatre to welcome any story, I sensed that many people had stories I would tremble to hear. I was also worried about disturbed or manipulative tellers. So to learn more about group process and deep stories, I had resolved to obtain training in psychodrama as part of my own development. In fact it all had come together, training at the Moreno Institute to better equip me to lead this new form of theatre, and a decision to invite certain people I met there to come to the group's first meeting.

One was Judy Swallow, with a masters in psychology, a deep acceptance of people, and an endlessly flexible face. She was to become a core member of the new group and eventually a worldwide trainer of the new approach (as well as a leader of the American psychodrama movement). There was Carolyn Gagnon, a neonatal nurse who was fearless on stage and off. They brought a friend with them, Vince Furfaro, a teacher with an infectious warmth and charm. He would listen to the teller's story with the same respect and love of life he brought to all natural creatures.

Others in the group were community members with varied backgrounds. We had Danielle Gamache, another teacher; Marko Whitely, a Vietnam veteran who worked as a plumber. We would add a psychotherapist named Gloria Robbins, whose wisdom about people helped us understand our tellers and ourselves; a community worker named Susan Denton (she initially worked for the police), whose wit and common touch would spark our performances; Bruce Mardiney, a humorous folk dancer and social worker; Pete Christman, a manager at IBM, who for years kept our financial records, and Michael Clemente, a talented actor, whose empathic eye was always on the underdog.

I did not reach out to local amateur community theatre aficionados. (In our semi-rural region there was virtually no professional theatre.) I mistrusted this community of self-identified actors, with their allegiance to the traditions of plays and musicals. I knew that I needed actors willing to face audiences as themselves as well as in a role, and I knew I needed a certain kind of maturity — people who would make a responsible contribution to a group that did not disband when the show's run was over. Additionally, I sensed, without yet being able to describe it, that we would be creating a specific aesthetic that would be closer to dance or mime than textual acting. An actor experienced in performing plays might have some production skills, but would he have the flexibility for our kind of ensemble theatre?

In fact over the years we took into the company a handful of community theatre actors, and invariably they did not work out. They were histrionic, or not good listeners, or resisted the demands of group life. Even so, I now wonder why I was so wary of trained actors. There had been my father the ex-actor's warnings when I was young ("actors are irresponsible"); there were the actors I met during my own short experience in the New York professional children's theatre (yearning for fame and fortune). Perhaps pulled by an idea I had of popular theatre, I favored "ordinary" citizens. And I knew very few legitimate actors, not traveling in those circles.

Slaughter the Pig

In those first rehearsals, attendance fluctuated. I was the believer, while the others were each waiting for proof that it really worked. As I stood before the troops, my own notebook in hand, I could feel their wariness, the gap between my commitment and theirs. I would not be daunted, however, especially with Jo at my side. I pushed us ahead. Each session we moved our bodies and voices; we exercised individually, in pairs, and all together. We worked on staging and keeping enactments crisp. We worked on finding the endings.

Our scenes had definite dramatic qualities, but there was a distinct feeling at the same time of being underwhelmed. The stories felt ordinary, and the enactments dull. Everything changed, however, after our sixth meeting. We had started a practice of allowing guests to come to one rehearsal a month as a way to give us a quasi-performance challenge. It was a visitor who told the last story that evening.

> *My father was a farm butcher, and he would be called to slaughter pigs and other animals. I went with him one day. I was holding my new little puppy in one hand and one of his knives in the other. When he began to slaughter the pig, I was so scared I jumped and cut myself badly. My dog barely escaped in one piece.*

After we acted out this story, for the first time everyone in the room felt the power of our approach, including the teller, who seemed to experience a deep catharsis. I was able to exhale deeply, thinking now maybe the doubters would be appeased. (One actor dropped out after that session, obviously not wanting to be part of a theatre of such strong emotion, regardless of its truthfulness to life.)

Through trial and error we slowly adopted certain "rules." One was not to start a scene before the narrator had finished telling. It was a first step toward creating what we would later label the "ritual."

Over the first few months basic terms suggested themselves. "Conductor" seemed usable for the facilitator figure, since it suggested interacting with audience and narrator and also a conduit (of flow, of attention, of energy). The "narrator" became the "teller." As for a name for the group, and for the approach as a whole, we sat around a table one day and in the end came up with "playback theatre." As in "We play your story back to you. Any story, big or small. From long ago or the present." We did not feel the name was particularly elegant, but it was the best we could do at the time. (How were we to know that it would not translate well into many other languages, where "playback" means lip synching?)

We drew inspiration from a mix of sources. The colorful Alwin

Nikolais dancers and experimental theatre director Joseph Chaikin influenced the development of our short forms, including what came to be called fluid sculptures and pairs, as well as our use of theatre lights and colored fabric as props. Our homespun appearance (white overalls over colored t-shirts) and willingness to sing simple folk and children's songs showed an affinity for popular theatre. The theatre-in-education movement spurred us to hold workshop segments as an interlude in early performances.

And of course there was our debt to psychodrama, the world headquarters of which was just down the road. We were very ready to correct or transform a scene, depending on whether the teller felt we had captured what she had told (we always checked after an enactment, asking the tellers if they had seen their story). We sometimes brought to the stage the double of a character ("Pick someone to be yourself and someone to play your timidity"). We invited the narrator to choose the main characters from the row of actors.

Many of these elements we would later drop or alter. For instance, we found that doubled characters for the most part did not work because they were too abstract and overtly psychological. The story world has a different way to show the same thing by inventing a character to combat or ally with the protagonist (such as Gretel and the witch, Jack and the giant, or Cinderella and her fairy godmother).

On the thirty-minute drive to our rehearsals, my stomach was often clenched in an aching knot. Remembering my extreme nervousness and excitement, the group's natural ambivalence, and my confused ambition (professional basis? giving one-third of our performances away for free?) — in short, recollecting the gulf between the dream and the reality, I am amazed at what playback theatre became. The vision contained a room, not a map of the world; a single theatre group, not hundreds. But perhaps an expanded view was implicit in the original image. For if a community here found playback theatre engaging, why not one there? If performers in one town could please and enlighten their fellow citizens by acting out their stories, then why couldn't actors in another town do the same?

Road Marker

Early in the new year of 1976 we started to perform for the public. We were still so green. But my secret hope was that if our work resonated with audiences, the actors would start believing.

The first performance took place in the church hall for family and friends. We were innocent of the fact that family audiences, with their long-standing conflicts, secrets, and hidden dynamics, can be among the most difficult. In fact Judy's six-year-old son told a story about a nightmare he had relating to his parents' imminent divorce. Judy was one of the actors. It was a delicate moment, a test of our allegiance both to intimacy and the ideal of positive personal outcomes.

For that first show we asked for donations from spectators. The box office, the record shows, totaled $11.80, a sum so small I am surprised I even recorded it.

Encouraged by the example of Werkteater in Holland and others, we would not be confined to traditional theatres. In April we performed at an academic conference. Could we engage graduate students as well as six-year-olds?

In this show a teller told another nightmare. But the circumstances were completely different. First of all, the audience was much larger, close to a hundred. Second, we had started in a bold and risqué manner, entering in street clothes, then retiring behind a screen, where we threw them off to saucy music in a kind of public strip, only to emerge in our clownlike playback gear. We undoubtedly triggered a light mood with these shenanigans, but there was no doubt that the audience, after a long day of intellectuality, wanted to play. When a woman teller began to tell of being sexually attacked (in her dream), the audience did not sober up. Why the teller told such a story in what seemed like such an unsympathetic setting, I have no idea. It may have been triggered by our sexy entrance. What I remember is my deep concern as the actors portrayed her story with full seriousness, only to have the audience laugh. We were not happy with this outcome, and it also showed us how much we had to learn.

In May we performed on the children's ward of the general hospital. Our stage was the play space at the center of the ward.

Many of the children watched from beds wheeled down the corridor. It was visiting hour, and parents were there, and of course some nursing staff as well.

The beginning felt like disaster. Dressed in our overalls, we had made our upbeat entrance (this time no public costume change). We sang a children's song. But when we asked for the first audience response, there was silence. I tried different questions. Nothing. The kids, ill and on medication, lacked the bounce and eagerness of other young audiences. The adults held back. The silence stretched.

Finally in response to one of my questions, one child made a small noise. He didn't say anything, just made this squeaking sound. I was ready to ignore it, but Vince jumped center stage, playing back the sound. Other actors joined him.

And that loosened the children up. The stories began to flow. We heard from a child about waiting alone to be taken into the operating room. A nurse told about spilling water on herself. A parent told about a tense drive to the hospital. We listened, and we played every story back.

Afterward there was a feeling of lightness in the room. The kids and their parents were smiling. I felt buoyed up. I could tell the actors felt the same. The halting start did not seem to matter. We had broken through a blanket of silence that kept people from sharing their inner lives with each other. They seemed to feel good about it. Perhaps this was how playback theatre was supposed to work.

Our ten performances in 1976 also took place in schools, outdoor festivals, and as box office theatre. Later we would extend this range to prisons, senior centers, and other community organizations. Slowly our confidence grew. Our open rehearsals evolved into monthly performances that we called our First Friday series. The audiences ranged from ten to eighty in size, averaging in the twenties. Despite the low numbers, someone always raised a hand to tell a story. Sometimes there was a hesitation, although never so long as on the hospital ward with ill children. But eventually a teller always came forth. And then another.

We often included a segment called "audience-up" in which

actors would leave the stage, creating space for audience members to take their place. We would then invite the next teller to tell, with audience actors performing the story. The purpose was to emphasize that everyone is an actor as well as a potential teller. It also called attention to the accessibility of playback theatre. These scenes worked surprisingly well. If we gradually dropped them, it was because the audience-up section was too much of an interruption to the actors' flow and concentration.

Along the way we got our taste of strange and challenging tellers, who told stories with hidden meanings inaccessible to our intuition and correspondingly difficult to play. We encountered tellers wanting to make us look weak and stupid. But these occasions were quite rare. Most who spoke up willingly responded to our invitation to co-construct a linked community story of individual everyday experiences. We also developed our sophistication in reading the signs for troubled tellers.

During our rehearsals, always so short-seeming, we built up our skills by reviewing performance moments and building up our understanding of the form. Our all-day Sunday practices allowed us time to go deeper into our own stories. I remember a secret Danielle told, a shattering event with a lover. It brought us closer to her, and as a younger member, I learned something about life. For Danielle, the experience seemed to lift a burden. In this way we learned to trust that our method could contain very serious, even traumatic stories, and still hold to the founding principle that the theatre be positive for the players.

By now there was a general sense that we were pursuing something worthwhile. Even so, before every rehearsal the phone would ring.

Actor: "I can't come tonight/today. I'm really sorry."

Me: "Oh, really? Why not?"

Actor:" I have a terrible cold"/ or "I'm just too tired from work"/ or "We just had a big fight, and I just don't have the strength."

Me: "You have to take care of yourself"/ or "We'll manage"/ or "Are you sure you wouldn't feel better coming and being with us?"

Each rehearsal I would end up counting—how many present, how many missing.

Music is so central to what a playback theatre performance became, but at the beginning we did not quite have the idea. Jo had played for It's All Grace, but she was not yet an improviser. It was not until an improvising keyboard player appeared eight months after the start that we introduced music. The first time he played with us, Marko told the following story:

I was walking along a road on duty in Vietnam. I came across a distance marker. So many kilometers to Hanoi, it said. So many to LA. So many to New York. There was no one else around at that moment, just me and the sign and the dirt road.

So short, this story. I did not ask for more, but simply accepted what Marko told. In the enactment one actor took to the stage, laden with imaginary rifle, pack, and equipment as the piano started to play a slow elegiac tune. The actor started walking from stage left to right. He raised his head. As he noticed the sign with its mention of home, the music built to a crescendo of notes encompassing anger, despair, and longing, then returned to the initial mournful theme. There was no monologue, no words at all. The actor continued walking. End of scene.

Everybody was moved. After this story, there was no question about the power of music to deepen the impact of the scenes. In fact, we felt one-armed without it. When the keyboard player left, we replaced him with a jazz guitarist, Ann Belmont. By this time, Jo had started to play music occasionally, and when Ann left, after about a year, Jo took over. Later studying at the Creative Music Studio in Woodstock, a center for improvisation and world music, Jo would become the consummate playback theatre musician, able to capture the heart of a story with instrument or voice (until she started Hudson River Playback Theatre and shifted mainly to conductor).

By the beginning of 1977 we were a company. The initial membership fluctuations had calmed, as did those begging-off phone calls before rehearsals. We had worked to develop our approach, tested it with different audiences, and felt it worked. Not always, of course, but often enough. Some of the actors had full-time jobs and were happy to continue performing playback theatre as an avocation. Jo and I did not. We had just had another baby, our daughter Madeline. I wanted more. It was time to build the organization and earn our living from our passion.

Chapter Four

Psychodrama Connection

"Don't hit me!"

I gasped. The speaker was Ann Hale, one of my teachers. She was role playing in a psychodrama. It dealt with a female client who was trying to escape the advances of her therapist. Ann had taken the role of the protagonist. When she came out with this seemingly out-of-context plea, I was stunned by its originality. The protagonist leapt back into her own role and reproduced the line. The moment opened up for her a previously buried part of her past.

How could someone be so spontaneous, I wondered. So insightful.

Ann is one of those persons.

It was from Zerka Moreno, from Ann as her assistant, and then later from the psychologist John Nolte that I learned the fine points of Moreno's system.

In 1975 I was working at the Moreno Institute, trading editing services for training and a small stipend. Our first rehearsal space, the church hall, was down the road from the Institute, and Zerka paid the first year's rent (she was enthusiastic about what she saw as our attempt to create another Theatre of Spontaneity, as Moreno had done in Vienna).

Moreno himself, the self-proclaimed genius and creator of psychodrama, was still alive when I attended my first training session in 1973, but he was no longer teaching. We learned his precepts from Zerka and Ann. Moreno's concept of spontaneity gave depth to my understanding of improvisation. The goal, he insisted, was not only to be creative and alive, but *appropriate* (responding to life's circumstances with appropriate flexibility). He also offered a sophisticated concept of group process, which focused on being open to *anyone's* contribution. I liked this philosophy.

My connection to the Institute was complicated by family events. My brother Matthew, whose hand I was always holding in spirit if not in fact, had died of heart failure earlier that year at the age of twenty-six, and in the aftermath, my mother left her marriage to my stepfather, Merlyn Pitzele. During the break-up he had started to attend open sessions of psychodrama with Zerka Moreno directing, and after J.L. Moreno died in 1974, the two became involved. Thus it was not a complete surprise when my unfulfilled requests for financial help to study at the Moreno Institute were suddenly met with a complete reversal. Not only did Zerka suddenly offer me a scholarship, but she even offered me a job. Merlyn and Zerka were to remain together. In time our children came to consider Zerka another grandmother, while I in certain circles became the "other Jonathan" (Zerka's only child being Jonathan Moreno). My stepbrother Peter Pitzele was also drawn into the psychodrama orbit, studying later at the Institute and going on to develop an innovative approach to bibliodrama. When some years after Moreno's death Zerka sold the Institute grounds and asked us to take anything we wanted, Jo and I chose his office chair, a nice piece with arms, high back, and rattan seat.

It is ironic that on my first visit I was ushered into the Moreno sitting room, where "Doctor" sat in his pajamas. He had a kind face and very big eyes. We exchanged a few words of small talk, and he gave me an autographed postcard of himself. "You will be like a son to me," he said. I had no idea what he was talking about and quickly lost the card. But his words turned out to be prophetic: who would imagine that his widow would take up with my stepfather?

No question, that first weekend training, which included a Saturday evening talk about Moreno's theatre experiments, helped trigger the idea for playback theatre some months later. I saw psychodrama as an exciting form of theatre — personal, intimate, honest, dramatic, unplanned. Sparks flew in my head.

But from the start my own theatre vision was distinct, both

from Moreno's Stegreiftheater and the therapeutic method that later emerged from it.

Playback theatre had a different purpose. Our aim was to bear witness, not to cure. Our focus was not on a patient (or client), but on the community. True, our embrace of personal narrative, including traumatic stories from childhood (hog butcher's son) and stories involving someone else present (child about his actor mother), exposed us from the start to the charge that playback theatre *was* therapy, even though we never thought that way ourselves. Not infrequently after a performance an audience member would approach one of us and say: "That was great. Thanks a lot. But tell me, is it really therapy?" Behind the remark lurked a criticism: "This is not theatre as I know it." Of course I always did my best to answer cheerfully. We all did. But I did not always feel so diplomatic inside, especially while the sweat was still drying from two hours under the lights. "Of course it's theatre!" I wanted to cry. "It's theatre. It's theatre. It's theatre!"

Another distinction centers on the aesthetic. Psychodrama, gestated in turn-of-the-century Europe, embraced conflict, *Sturm und Drang*. It was a fierce approach. I remember watching protagonists on that first visit throw metal chair seats at a wall to express their anger. It made such a tremendous racket. I could barely stay in the room.

Skating by Torchlight

No one was fiercer than Zerka Moreno. She was a master at the drama of psychodrama, in part because she pushed protagonists to their limits. "Let's go there," she would say, referring to a long-suppressed corner of the protagonist's psyche.

"I can't," he would reply, terrified.

"Go!"

"No, it's too much!"

"If not now, you never will do it. Go!"

Zerka invariably prevailed, and the protagonist, after going through an ordeal, invariably felt relief.

Playback theatre, in contrast, is less interventionist. We do not try to pop the lid off the pot. This gentleness also distinguished us, by the way, from much experimental theatre of the time, inspired by Artaud's "going for the bone." Our stance was Eastern rather than European. We welcomed whatever came.

With my feel for story and reading people, psychodrama skills came easily to me, and once I completed the training, I succeeded in obtaining some work as a psychodrama trainer. In the profession, however, I remained an outlier, since I identified as a theatre person, not a psychotherapist. The majority of psychodramatists regarded me similarly and held me at bay. The company's applications to perform at annual psychodrama conferences, for instance, were accepted some years and rejected in others, in spite of the hefty crowd we drew there.

Some time later (1996) I was invited to Israel for the purpose of leading a closing playback theatre plenary session at an international psychodrama conference. My event was to have a grand title that included the words "peace" and "spirituality." I was excited. As the weeks passed I remember noting that where I might expect confirmations and communications about final arrangements, instead there was silence. When I finally asked what was going on, the reply was a shocker. It turned out they had decided to uninvite me and then omitted telling me. No reason was given. Evidently the organizing committee had decided they did not want playback theatre.

My ticket bought and paid for, I went anyway. I ignored the wishes of students that we stage guerrilla playback in the psychodrama corridors. I did attend that final plenary, now led by another. I was stunned to observe that in a crowd of well over a hundred participants, only three Arabs were present. I had been naive not only about Israeli psychodramatists' interest in playback theatre, but also about their commitment to meaningful peace. I breathed a sigh of relief that I had not been coopted into leading the session (playback theatre would flourish in Israel, and later be independently taken up in surrounding Arab regions, but with little connection to psychodrama).

Not every psychodramatist disrespected our work. Zerka stood behind us. Ann Hale became a playback company founder, along with many psychodramatists who would develop a decades-long commitment to our new method. One was René Marineau, a Canadian professor of psychology who became Moreno's biographer. He saw us perform at one of those conferences and invited Jo and me to introduce playback theatre to his graduate students. We worked with them in a studio above his garage, located in the village of Yamachiche in rural Québec, with the snow thick on the surrounding fields and forests. On Saturday night instead of a work session René hosted a "soirée," a kind of talent night that he claimed was an old local tradition (he came from a large family, he said, and the custom in that isolated region was to entertain themselves). I loved this kind of evening, and clearly the students did, too. René is as comfortable in his sugar shack making maple syrup as he is in his office seeing patients, and he is known for hosting skating parties for his students on the river that crosses his land.

Today after so many years, playback theatre is generally accepted in the psychodrama field, in part due to the influence of psychodramatists like Ann, René, and Judy Swallow, who adapt it for their work. While it has been important to me over the years to make clear playback theatre's distinct identity, at bottom I am pleased to possess Moreno's chair, which sits in our living room to this day.

CHAPTER FIVE

The Young Company

In those first years we were exuberant. After rehearsals, we went to the diner just to prolong our time together. We went on picnics in our free time, even hot tubs (after all, it was the 1970s). We were constantly inventing new forms, trying them in performance, later dropping them as inadequate in one way or another. One was a form we called a walkabout involving actors walking diagonally across the stage. Another form that made a brief appearance we called a baklava, but I can't even remember what that was now. Their names reflected our spirit.

Even though the number of structures we relied on in performance stayed small (fluid sculptures, pairs, and the longer scenes, or stories), I showed up with a big sheet before each performance detailing the planned order: entrance, performers' intro, fluids, audience intros (to each other), stories, pairs, more stories, ending. I enjoyed the secret echo of the maestro in commedia dell'arte who nailed his *carnovaccio* to the wall so that performers would know the order of the routines.

We worked on our use of cloth, the fabrics of different colors, shapes, and texture that we used to add color to a scene. The cloth was easy to use poorly (a big piece of blue around the waist as a skirt), and very hard to use well (the piece stretched out on the stage that represented the long journey undertaken by an African-American teller determined to earn her PhD, against which the teller's actor, and those playing the impediments, embodied the scene).

Whenever we could we used lighting and the skills of a light board operator to provide an improvisational counterpoint of color.

The music evolved. Jo learned how to play effective "setting up" music, that brief period following the conductor's interview while the actors were taking their places for the coming scene. (We spurned the practice of a pre-enactment huddle, common in improvisation, because we felt it did not in fact increase the chance of creative ensemble work).

In our performances Jo's position surrounded by her instruments stage left mirrored mine as conductor stage right, with the teller's chair beside me and the actors sitting upstage center. Wherever we performed, we maintained this onstage embrace of the audience.

It was a Saturday morning in spring, and we had gathered to take part in a Japanese tea ceremony. Actually it was a lesson in tea ceremony. The teacher was far from a native-born Japanese. In fact, she was an American woman who had taken on a Hindu name. Let's call her Lakshmi. How much Lakshmi actually knew about tea ceremony was anyone's guess. She had instructed us to bow each time she bowed, and we quickly started giggling. She bowed every thirty seconds, it seemed. The situation was not helped by the husband of one of our actors, who showed up in full samurai costume. He was not giggling, which made us all the more giddy. Each time she bowed, we lowered our heads in straggly response, holding back guffaws. That's how things were in those days.[6]

We did have a legitimate reason for trying out this bowing stuff. We had realized that in playback theatre a good deal of time was spent not in the dramatic enactment but *in between.* There was the social interaction part, where the conductor spoke to the audience and invited them to tell something. But there was also another part, those moments before and after the embodiment of the story: how we sat on the cubes listening to a teller, how we entered into an enactment, how we positioned ourselves just afterward. Attention to this overall structure helped us develop what we came to call the *ritual* of playback theatre. The art of playback had no rules; it depended on play and freshness. But the ritual had rules and had to be done consistently. Like all rituals, it provided a kind of safety and could contain deep experience. These two aspects, the art and the ritual, seemed to pull in opposite directions. One was inventive and quick; the other slow and shamanic.

Thus in spite of our playfulness, we were trying to expand our skills in what felt like uncharted territory. One of our listening exercises even consisted of silently "sending" stories to each other, then sharing what we "heard." It was hard to tell if these and other activities were a waste of time. But we forged ahead.

Greater command of the ritual helped with our ability to hear the story behind the story, a skill we came to call "deep listening." Not surprisingly such attention spilled over to our company life. We learned to notice when one was silent and give her space to talk. Some of us were able to gradually discard life-long habits of needing to be seen and heard above the others. We learned that being in the company took considerable effort, especially to constantly practice the empathy and mutual respect that we promoted with audiences. Some newcomers didn't stick because it was just too much. In fact, it was not long before our larger numbers at start-up pared down to eight members.

One day as we were about to start one of our First Friday box office shows I noticed a new couple in the audience. Afterward they came up to us, but not to ask "Was it therapy?" Instead, speaking with a European accent, they said they were visiting New York City (two hours away) to see theatre. "Somebody told us to come up here if we wanted to see the best impressionistic mime in town." The best impressionistic mime! I had never considered what we did as mime—after all, we used words—but it was true we strove to create theatre around, under, in between, and instead of the words. The arrival of these strangers meant that word was getting around. There was something new on the theatre scene, and it was us.

Pilot for the Countrywide Tour

Despite our messy and unruly experiments, we took pains to dress our new theatre company in respectable clothing. In 1977 we lined up a board of directors and filed for legal not-for-profit status. We opened a bank account. We started to publish annual reports. We networked. And we looked for institutional sources of funding.

The first opportunity came from the local association of senior citizens, which engaged us to do playback at their centers. The following year a group of agencies asked us to perform as part of a year-long program honoring the 300th anniversary of the locality. These performances resulted in an illustrated booklet called "Stories of Dutchess County." With visions of crossing the continent in a bus or big van with "Playback Theatre" painted boldly on the side, we saw it as a pilot for a nationwide tour to be called "Stories of America."

In 1978 we began a many-year relationship with the county youth bureau, offering playback theatre to young people. For this program we used a performance/workshop model, in which we placed as much emphasis on acting as on telling. The program taught skills of self-expression, listening, and building empathy. The format of each meeting was to do lots of warm-ups and exercises, leading up to a short period of playback theatre.

During this period, inspired by my children, I worked as a clown in a small weekend circus, and somehow I managed to parlay this into a job with the government department of planning and transportation. My name was Bussy Travels. I wore a red hat, blue top, flaring orange and red trousers, a very long scarf, and huge white shoes. My joyful face was graced with the poetic touch of a light-blue tear sliding down one cheek. Bussy's task was to ride the public buses of Poughkeepsie, as well as to appear in malls and march in parades.

The department hired us to perform playback theatre at some of their conferences, and when they saw how well the audience responded, they subsequently encouraged us to apply for a federal grant. This was not strictly playback theatre, but role playing to help teach recently deinstitutionalized individuals how to deal with public transportation. We took it on because it allowed five company members to go on paid contract. Although the total amount was small, just $3,160 per actor per year, it was enough to ask them to be primarily available for playback theatre work. We all lived on very little in those days.

These opportunities were in the oral history, youth services and rehabilitation fields. Our applications to arts councils met with a much cooler response.

In 1981 we hired a part-time managing director, and in the following year rented our first office. Underlying these efforts was a determination to say Yes to opportunity, develop a track record, show that we could fulfill our promises, get business done. Ours might be a different kind of theatre, but we would present it in a conventional-looking package. From the outset, even while I idealistically told the actors that I wanted them to be able to "live in the world," never doing playback theatre "full-time," I sought to build an organization that could compete in conventional terms with professional community-based theatres.

We were proud of our new office. It represented a big step forward. There was now a place, a phone, and someone to answer that phone. We also established a performance base at a local museum, the Mid Hudson Arts and Science Center in Poughkeepsie, New York, which became the home for our rehearsals and monthly box office performances. Our space at the museum suited us — on the second floor, above the exhibits — a spacious room with a good floor, big windows, and a balcony.

Sometime during this period I read an article in *The New York Times* stating that the average professional actor earned less than $3,000 per year from acting. I was proud, too, that our actors on contract were actually doing better than that.

Playing the Nimrod

Five years after our start we had well over a hundred performances behind us — performances for organizations, conference and festival-goers, children and their parents, adolescents, the elderly, those living with intellectual differences, the incarcerated, and the public-at-large. We had built an organization. We had an office.

Most importantly, we had learned that audience members were quite willing to raise a hand and tell their story. In fact, they were often eager. Although their numbers were never large, they laughed, they cried, they clapped. Many came again and again. Observers from abroad sometimes reacted with skepticism, "Well, yes. This is America. You are all so extroverted here." However, we would soon learn that the readiness to tell one's story would turn out to be more than a product of American exhibitionism.

One day in 1979 an unskeptical foreigner came up to us after a conference performance and declared, "I want to bring you to Australia!" A professor, he was able to pull it off, and eight months later four of us traveled to Australia and New Zealand to give nineteen days of performances and workshops. We met wonderful, talented, original people there. In Melbourne, our first stop, we taught in the workspace of a woman named Zandi who lived in a converted auto repair shop. She had aluminum foil on the walls and an oversized hot tub. Our concept was to hold a multiday workshop in each city, then select some of the participants to perform with us. This risky plan worked. Each of our three performances at Melbourne State College drew more of an audience, until the house sold out.

On that final evening before the show we noticed a line of tape placed over an entire row with the legend "faculty." That none of them came up afterward to praise us did not matter (we could assume their preference was scripted theatre). But at least they attended. Later in Sydney we performed after hours at the famous Nimrod Theatre, again to a full house, and we even had to add a second show. Such popular success was so exhilarating that once back home I could not sleep for days.

I ended our first five years proud and perky, writing in our annual report (1980): "To set about to create a full-time theatre company, especially outside the city, is an ambitious goal. However, I envision a day when Playback talent and teaching personnel will be widely in demand, and students will come — to Dutchess County — from the world over to learn our techniques." My prediction the following year was no less ambitious: "The company will perform in the Mid-Hudson (NY) region, nationally, and abroad."

Why not? We were well established at home, funded by the regional arts council, if not the more prestigious ones. We were hired by many community agencies. We had recently started training classes for adults and children.

I was convinced that what we were doing was groundbreaking and artistically relevant. It was totally spontaneous. It centered on personal narrative. It demanded empathy. It championed the people's voice. New York City would acclaim us. We would travel the length of the United States with our Stories of America. Even more, we would travel the world, using the workshop/performance format honed in Australia to seed new companies everywhere.

CHAPTER SIX

Performance

Here is a typical performance of the original playback theatre company:

It was four in the afternoon. Hot water from the shower rolled off my head and shoulders as I thought about the upcoming show and my first words to the audience. Did I want something funny? Something serious? How about mentioning the research of my professor Albert Lord in the mountains of Yugoslavia, and the storytellers there who could memorize a ten- or twelve-hour tale? It was a nice angle. We do not have to memorize anything to be a playback teller, I could say. And a story of a few minutes' length is as good as one lasting a day (or a night), I could say. Yes, that was it.

When the time came, Jo and I made sure the babysitter had all instructions. We loaded instruments, cloth props, and wooden boxes into the car. We made sure we had the ticket box, with some small bills for change, and blank paper for the mailing list. I hated having to keep track of these things as I was getting ready to perform. But it had to be done. Frowning, I took the wheel as we headed for the Mid-Hudson Arts and Science Center, our home performance space.

It was an hour and a half before showtime. The other actors had arrived on time for once and were setting up the space. Jo was tuning her violin, while I was still focusing on Albert Lord and exactly what words I would use to evoke him. I directed a series of warm-ups, and then we put on dance music.

Cloistered in the inner room, we could see the audience entering the hall. "Not so many!" I said, disappointed. "It's enough," said Michael. Judy was talking to Gloria and Susan about a new place to buy shoes.

It was time. Dennis dimmed the lights, brought them up high, and Jo entered playing. We had chosen our no-nonsense opening. The actors entered briskly. I started my intro, the moment I cherished and feared. "Good evening," I said. "Welcome! (I paused). But I have to tell you right off. We have no show." Titters of laughter. I walked to the other side of the stage, doing a strange jump halfway, as I explained our no-preparation, full-improvisation credo. "We have memorized nothing, not so much as a pismire," I said. Strong laughter. I was connecting. Where did "pismire" come from? Actually I knew. From Walt Whitman ("I believe a leaf of grass is no less than the journey-work of the stars / And the pismire is equally perfect, and a grain of sand, and the egg of the wren.") But I didn't care. And what ever happened to Albert Lord?

"How are you this evening? How was your day today?" I asked the audience.

"I mowed my lawn. It took hours," a man replied.

"Watch!" I said, and the actors took center stage for the first enactment. I took a breath. For me, it had been a good beginning, needing very few words — despite being totally different than I had expected. More short forms followed. A woman told about working in her office. Another woman told about getting a clear bill of health from her doctor. A third said her partner was smoking again among his friends. Each narrative was enacted. I noticed the actors doing better with each successive short form.

When the time came for a longer story, I saw two hands go up, a woman's and a man's. I felt drawn to the woman, but I was conscious that the recent tellers had all been women. So I invited the man.

Almost at once, I suspected that I had made a mistake. As he sat he shifted his chair so that he was facing the actors more directly. I shifted my chair to parallel his.

"What is this? Monkey see, monkey do?" he said, in a directly challenging way.

"Just trying to make sure I can see your face," I answered.

"All you have to do is listen to my story," he answered. I could feel his prickliness, his unwillingness to let me conduct him.

"What is your story about?" I asked.

"It's about what's happening right now," he answered. One of those tellers, I say to myself. A challenger. "I want you people to do that."

"What?"

"What's happening right now."

"Well," I said. "We're not going to do that. We are not in fact here just to follow orders. Who is in your story?" I ask, my tone changing.

His tone suddenly changes, as well. "My father," he says. "He was a definite bastard."

"Pick one of the actors to be your father," I say at once. As soon as he does, pointing to Bruce, I knew he had finally accepted the ritual. At the same time, he dropped all pugnacity. His story turned out to be a tale of a teenager craving acceptance from a withholding, probably depressed father. After the enactment is over, the teller laughs weakly. "Yes," he says. "That's what it's been like."

"Thank you," I said, as he returned to his seat. I took a breath, relieved that this first teller did not get the better of me.

I cast my eye around the audience as I invite another teller. There is a small voice inside me that is asking why there aren't more people there (the audience numbers somewhere between twenty and thirty). But I remain mostly in the moment. Again, two hands go up. I take a woman with wavy hair. Her story is about buying her first house and feeling grown-up in a new way, despite the fact that her parents are helping financially. The interview unfolds smoothly, and I send it over to the actors, who portray the story with sensitivity.

The third narrative, another house story, is a surprise. A woman tells about a fire. Her husband and friends let a cigarette burn at the end of a drinking party while she is out with a girlfriend. The actors do a strong job of building up to the climax of the scene, with Danielle and Michael, as the sluggish men, for a long time ignoring the growing flames portrayed by Susan using the cloth, as Judy and Gloria shop together innocently on the other side of the stage. Susan as the fire speaks menacingly: "I will destroy it all!" The men in the room drink and laugh, oblivious. They give and take the focus from the women shopping. It is a skill we have practiced, and from my conductor's chair I note the actors' success with satisfaction. The tension mounts until the men notice the fire and suddenly jump into terrified action. "Do you think this looks good on me?" asks one of the women from the shopping area, as the scene suddenly ends.

It is so simple-seeming, this playing back, but I knew it was not simple, and I appreciated that the actors portrayed the action with the needed emotional power.

"Are you now back in the house?" I asked, imagining that audience members might also be wondering. "Just two weeks ago," she said. "Thank you," I say, as the teller returns to her seat.

Since the impact of the previous enactment was strong, I decided to change our plan, which called for using the lively pairs form after three stories, instead calling for responses to the fire story, which we enact with fluid sculptures and music. Tellers mention feelings of fear, anger at a spouse, remembering their own disasters, being away from home when something happens.

As I invited the last story of the evening, I was ready for any story, and I felt the actors were, too. I felt fully present, a precious feeling.

A man half-raised his hand. I sensed something from him, and I nod, inviting him to come to the teller's chair. "It's my dad's birthday today," he says, as he sits. It turns out his father would have been eighty-two years old had he lived. "He was a good man," says the teller. "Give me an example," I say. The teller pauses. "Well, this is a silly example," he says, "but we used to go fishing. I was seven or eight. And every time he caught a fish he would do this secret movement with his back to me, and suddenly the fish was on my line and I was catching the fish. He would praise me and clap me on the back. I knew what was happening, of course, but I felt great nonetheless. He made me feel like a king." "Yes, a good man," I say. The actors do the scene, full boisterous playfulness and pretense, but at the end father and son just look at each other, giving space for Jo to play a melody of love.

Then came a final moment of both characters laughing with joy and appreciating their (mutually caught) fish, and the scene—and the evening—was over. As the music played, we slowly stood and took center stage for our bow. The audience clapped heartily—for us, a golden moment.

It had been a good show. I had done my part and had a chance to do what I loved—be in the unplanned moment, exercise my clownish self, and guide the audience through the risky waters of conflict and strong feeling. This time there are no admiring guests from New York City to stir my ambitions. Nor are there interlocutors with false smiles asking, "What is this, anyway?" Instead there is just the buzz of conversation—people making contact with us and each other, talking about the stories of the evening, sharing one of their own.

In the time of the original company we did not understand about what later came to be called the "red thread," the connections binding the stories. But we could sense the obvious. It was a performance that had an organic feel to it, as if indeed there was in the end one communal "play," rather than a series of individual tales. The first story of a son whose father failed to love him was completed by a last story of a father who knew just how to love his son, and stories about betraying, irresponsible men (smoking in secret, letting a house fire start) were answered by one about a caring, loyal man.

It was enjoyable chatting with the audience afterward, mainly because our part was now done. We could rest easy. The stories had been strong; they had carried us along. I would feel their power for days.

Chapter Seven

Struggles

Standing in the back, dressed in black, unsmiling, he was hard not to notice, especially because the entire audience numbered no more than forty people. We had been warned that the New York State Arts Council was sending an "auditor," or reviewer, to evaluate our work, and I guessed it was him. When I made a joke, the audience laughed. But the man in black remained stony-faced. The performers were in form, eliciting much applause, but his dour expression never changed. What a disaster, I thought. Imagine our surprise when he joined us for a bite after the show and said that he liked what we were doing. "This is the roots of theatre," he proclaimed. We were elated. But it is not the end of the story. After waiting months to hear from the Arts Council, confident that after the auditor's positive report we had a fighting chance, I phoned their office. "There is no report," they said. "He never turned one in. We never heard from him again."

In the end we did not get the money. We knew from the start it had been a long shot, since previously when I had met with the head of the theatre program he had told me that we had a "guideline problem." Our work was not product-focused enough to be called theatre, he said. But the reaction of the man in black had been so positive! And then he had disappeared! What did it all mean?

We were bewildered.

When we applied a few years later to the National Endowment for the Arts, another auditor came. He spent three days with us. This time he submitted his report. Again we did not get the money.

I believed ardently that our work deserved serious attention from arts councils. Perhaps we were just too innovative, too border-crossing for the restricted vision of these official bodies. Without question there was disdain among the cognoscenti for nonscripted approaches. How often, for example, was circus reviewed, or mime? Even the theatre critic for our local paper balked at reviewing playback theatre. "I need to read the script beforehand," he claimed. We might have done better in Canada, Australia, or Austria, which accepted community-based approaches, but we were here in the United States.

We seemed to gain more acceptance from the social service sector than the arts sector. So we bent with the wind. There was the local mental health association and the youth bureau. Then there was our federal grant from the county transportation department to teach coping skills. But what we hoped would provide income to elevate us to a new level of professionalism turned out to be a trap.

What we could not imagine, and did not have the foresight to research beforehand, was the slowness of the federal payment schedule—up to a year after completion of the work. We needed the money right away, and to have to wait months and months! This delay almost sank us, defeating the purpose of accepting the grant—providing funds to do our core playback work—and causing us all, me especially as the one most responsible, unmeasurable stress.

In fact, even though we lived very simply, the financial pressure was so great on our young family that for the only time in my entire working career, I took a regular job, filling in for an English professor on sabbatical. As I made the hundred-mile commute to my enforced employment in the pre-dawn gloom, my heart was heavy with the feeling that fate seemed stacked against us.

Falling Short

If you look over our annual budgets year after year, what stands out is the perennial shortfall of the reality compared to our estimates. We always did worse than we planned for. Something was getting in the way. Whatever the external barriers, it is not hard also to see internal reasons why we fell short.

The first was an ambivalence toward the idea of being "professional." I wanted it — and I didn't.

Let me tell you about that first office of ours. We rented a section of an empty factory in Poughkeepsie, a river city that had known better times. The cost was low. The space was unrenovated as well as cavernous. You had to walk for many minutes, steps echoing against distant walls, to reach our desks. In winter we crouched under sheets of plastic to try to keep close to our electric heaters, We wore gloves with cut-away fingers. We could never hold business meetings there. It was too frigid. We could barely work there ourselves.

Yet I was proud of this office. We were utilizing unused space. We were operating close to the earth, camping rough in the urban jungle. We were spending mere pennies.

Did we want to be businesslike, or not?

There was also a serious flaw in our business model. At the time I don't think I thought in terms of business models. We had a budget, but not a sound plan for earning the income we projected, hoping that shortfalls would be made up by pie-in-the-sky grant support. Ours was an intimate theatre, calling for small audiences of fifty, one hundred, two hundred at most. But to earn significant income from ticket sales requires large audiences. Furthermore, hearkening back to the "roots of theatre," as the man said, our small-town location meant an even smaller audience base than would have been possible, say, in any large city. Our chance for partnerships and projects was also correspondingly less than if we had located in a major metropolis (as did many later playback companies).

There was in addition our familylike ethos. The first question that the auditor from the National Endowment for the Arts asked me, as we sat in our second office, a perfectly hospitable space in a respectable downtown building (thank goodness), was "Tell me about the first time you fired an actor." In retrospect, this was a good question. "I've never fired an actor!" I replied, shocked, explaining that we did things differently. It was true, we did do things differently, needing our internal process to be as humanistic as our performance process. Nevertheless, I felt uneasy in my indignation, because I knew deep in my heart there were times when I *should* have fired an actor, but didn't. How could I fire one of the ones who had followed me so bravely, when the idea was a mere whisper and a dream?

At the core of the concept of professional enterprise lies the idea of decision-making based on achievement rather than personhood. Admittedly this question becomes especially delicate when the product is personhood itself (in the form of people's real stories). Even so, I remember times when we went too far—taking into the company, for example, the partner of someone we wanted as a way to make it easier for that candidate to say Yes. But the partner, while expressing interest (undoubtedly pushed by the mate), lacked skill or motivation.

Taking up our federal grant gave us a test of our values that I cannot say we passed. Five of the company were invited to sign contracts, while the others continued to participate on an avocational basis. The result was an awkward split. Even though we all initially agreed on the division, one part became much more active, getting more practice and getting paid for their efforts. We had one shoe off and one shoe on, an inner and an outer group. We had compromised our core unity for money.

No Peanuts in the Shooting Gallery

While I may have wanted to be recognized, we certainly did not cater to the cultural elites. Stronger was an interest in bringing playback theatre to those whose stories, we imagined, were less heard: the imprisoned, the disabled, the very old, the very young. I do not remember articulating at the time a clear rationale for this interest in performing for groups positioned on the margins of society, but what Professor Heinrich Dauber writes about us in Gathering Voices rings true: "two contemporary movements of the seventies come together: on the one hand, the culture of political resistance, as expressed through 'pedagogy of liberation' and the connected fight against the 'culture of silence.'"7

I do remember the choice-making process at the time of opening our first office in 1981. We rejected New Paltz, the village of 5,000 where we lived, a steadfastly middle-class, comfortable, cozy college town, for struggling Poughkeepsie, a nearby city of 30,000, with large pockets of alienated citizens.

Fueled by the same concern for those less fortunate that had drawn three of us, Judy, Jo, and myself, to volunteer for service abroad in our youth, we were an all-white, predominantly middle-class group reaching out to individuals whose background was less privileged than ours.

It is of course a laudable impulse to have a sympathetic interest in others, especially when the prevailing attitude is so often mistrust, hostility, and dehumanization. But there was a major problem in congruence. Our faces on stage looked so different from many of our tellers.

Heather Robb, a playback colleague from Australia and France trained in clowning and commedia dell'arte, stood up at an international gathering to criticize our vague concept of "service" as condescending and hypocritical. Heather mistrusted altruism as a motivation, preferring instead that we drop our pose of humility ("we are here for you") for an open admission of self-interested ambition ("we're here to make a name for ourselves and because we are paid"). I have mixed feelings about her critique. But certainly at the time my views were unformed. In fact I titled my book about theatre *Acts of Service* without ever clearly defining in its pages what I meant.

I remember being an actor in a performance at a women's prison, where to our surprise the inmates were not grateful to have us perform for them. One told a story of being at a "shooting gallery." Ignorant of the term, which referred to drugs, I pictured a fair or penny arcade and acted it out accordingly. They all laughed in scorn. On another occasion some years later we performed at a school in New York City. There was not a white face in the young audience (meaning this school was totally unintegrated). This time the students did not hold back, showing no hesitation to share their stories with us (one including a shooting at an after-school party). Yet by now I had started to feel the awkwardness of middle-aged white suburban performers enacting the stories of urban nonwhite, mostly immigrant teenagers.

An understanding of the full implications of a commitment to social change grew slowly. At the time we did not think about the narrow demographic range of our own group. Nor did we put an effort into building relationships with those community groups that represented the people we hoped to reach.

Outlier's Tale

It is the night before one of our First Friday public performances in Poughkeepsie at the Arts and Science Center. We are rehearsing. An African-American man, rough-dressed, comes in off the street, unusual because the museum is not open and our space is on the second floor. We can smell alcohol. He does not say much, at least that we can make sense of. What to do? We invite him to sit down and get warm while we continue with our work. We are not aware how much he is noticing.

But the next night, once our show is under way, he comes again. He sits in the audience for a short time, then when I invite the next teller, he approaches the chair. His story was not fully coherent, as I remember, but we enacted it as best we could. He seemed pleased, although I could sense unease from the public. Soon after, he wandered out as he had wandered in.

The show that this man off the street attended happened to be the one evaluated by the auditor from the National Endowment. Was this rambling, disjointed tale, and our struggle to find its kernel onstage, the reason our grant application was rejected? I imagine it was. It was certainly a weak point in our stage work that evening.

We were advised more than once to avoid such pitfalls, to exert more control, to find ways to reject "difficult" tellers. After all, they could bring down a show. But I never felt susceptible to this kind of suggestion. The premise of playback theatre is that we are ready to play *anybody's* story, and if a person who may be homeless, paralyzed, gay, or brown-skinned feels trusting enough to tell us his or her story, that has always been a tribute rather than a curse. The failure in those first years lay not in the openness of our invitations, but in our skill in integrating such tellers and their stories with the rest of the audience. If we deserved to be turned down for that grant, it was not because we had welcomed the man off the street, but because we did not know how to listen to him properly and bring the rest of the audience to a place where they, too, were willing to hear his story.

O.P.

Reviewing my role as an administrator of the original company, a puzzling question emerges. I had a clear hope for support from theatre funders, and to that end, we established the necessary practices (nonprofit legal structure, audited financial statements, and professional management). Yet there was a strange lack of follow through, especially when we were turned down. Our original application to the New York State Council on the Arts was rejected under murky circumstances — the auditor disappeared — but I never challenged them. We reapplied only once, four years later. Nor did we ever apply to the National Endowment for the arts more than once. If we were ahead of our time, that was all the more reason to reapply year after year, to show the viability of what we were doing. Why not find out why the theatre professors at Melbourne State College did not come backstage to congratulate us after our show in their theatre? Why not engage with them?

Making a decision to mount performances in New York City as a way to gain exposure, we negotiated with an Off-Off-Broadway theatre, but we dropped it after three shows there, ostensibly because we found the audience self-serving. Why give up so soon?

The best explanation lies in my own ego. I was hamstrung by what Ernest Becker calls the "narcissistic inflation" that befalls many founders, in which they confuse their own identities with their projects. Becker calls this syndrome the Oedipal Project (O.P.).[8] Even though it was the theatre that was being turned down, and not myself, I could not help taking the rejections personally. Each one chipped away at my core, and I hunkered down defensively, huddling under the plastic sheeting in our frigid office rather than resolutely go back out and insist we deserved another chance.

Despite a genuine penchant for collaboration, this confusion also affected my relations with the performers. We were often introduced at a conference or organizational event as "Jonathan

Fox and his team." The poster announcing our work in Australia featured a drawing of a fox with the headline, "Jonathan Fox is coming!" After not too long, the actors rebelled. We are an ensemble, they said, not just an appendage of you. The problem was not mine. I had not created this urge for a star, this exaggeration. And yet it took me a long time to effectively counter it. While I agreed with the actors, at the same time deep down I liked being singled out. To bring the company into the world had taken such an effort, and I wanted whatever recognition I could get.

The perception that it was "Jonathan's company" was especially unfair to Jo, who participated actively from the first moment of playback theatre's life. Our talents complemented each other. I was an initiator, she a meticulous pursuer. My skills lay in the interpersonal moment, hers in building artistic excellence; for years I was the conductor to stage right; she the musician to stage left; I used spoken words, she the cadences of her voice and violin.

Yet there was a paternalistic smell to this partnership. My talents tended to be noticed and recognized, while hers, as costumer, songwriter, designer, and writer, as well as musician, tended to remain unnoticed. Case in point: "Jonathan Fox is coming" (and she was the one who came from Down Under). For some years this imbalance remained unaddressed, but when we started to teach together, the problem rose starkly to the surface. Were we sharing leadership, or was she my underling? How to integrate what she called my "charismatic" style and her quieter, more restrained approach? I was used to taking the focus, and I was not comfortable sitting on the sidelines.

During the 1970s and 1980s gender relations were in upheaval all around us, and it caught us up, too. This was a good thing, but it was not easy for either of us, especially since part of the historical problem was institutionalized patterns of privilege and inferiority. To avoid suffocation, Jo would strike out on her own, founding Hudson River Playback Theatre, where she could thrive as artistic director, conductor, actor, and musician.

At a certain point Jo and I agreed to publicly correct the history. We asked colleagues in their teaching and writing to acknowledge us as co-founders. Even now, years later, we have to deal with laggard notices, which tout the Jonathan without the Jo.

The Fox/Salas Clan

Jo was not the only member of our family to become involved in playback theatre. Our daughter Hannah was almost five when the original company started. A few of us had small children in those years, and as a way to include them we decided to hold children's classes on Saturday mornings. This continued for four or five years. At matinee performances we would cede the stage to the kids from the older class, who, full of concentration and proud in their special t-shirts, would enter to enact the next story. Hannah took part.

When many years later she said she wanted to practice playback, we welcomed her intention, but said she would have to complete all the requirements of the School of Playback Theatre, which had by then been established. Despite her unique position as the daughter of the founders, she agreed, fulfilling all requirements and graduating in 2000. She became the founding artistic director of Big Apple Playback Theatre in New York City, integrating graduate theatre studies, experience from directing a playback group in Oregon, and a background in movement and dance.[9]

Some years later Jo's sister Janet Salas and her husband Peter Pfundt became involved in playback theatre in Germany. Our second daughter, Maddy, incorporated playback theatre in social psychology research for her doctoral dissertation.

It is somewhat strange to see my family members follow in my footsteps. The challenge is to see the other person as herself. Fortunately each has her own distinct interest and specialty.

In 2005 an amazing thing happened: at the German-speaking playback theatre gathering that year in Vienna, the organizers wanted Jo and me to anchor a playback theatre performance.

"We don't have a team," we said.

"You're Jonathan and Jo. Just select people," they replied.

We demurred. We did not want, nor had the time, to select and rehearse a team. Furthermore we knew it would stir up a hornet's nest of jealousy and criticism if we without warning cherry-picked colleagues for this task. The organizers obtusely insisted. So finally, as a kind of defiance, we agreed, but said we would pick the other performers by lot from among anyone who wanted to join us. The next morning in front of the hundred-plus participants our host pulled five names out of a hat. Against all odds, two of the five were our sister and brother-in-law, Janet and Peter. We trusted in the spontaneity of our choosing process. Some witnesses to that performance in Vienna said the lottery had to have been rigged. But we did not cheat. A combination of genuine enthusiasm and fate brought our family together onstage that day, and we embraced the opportunity.*

The Fifth Wall

Frustrated by my inability to gain more recognition for the original company and its work, I sought individual avenues. In 1982 I applied for a grant from the National Endowment for the Humanities for a study of Post Literary Theatre. I applied for a Guggenheim Fellowship. These and other similar initiatives met with no success. Getting up very early in the morning and writing in our unfinished basement, I completed a book, *Acts of Service*. It was my attempt to argue for playback's legitimacy despite its standing apart from literary theatre. I wrote it on an early computer, where the convenience of being able to categorize and sort all my notes was offset by the terror of making a mistake and losing a week's work. After twenty-five rejections, I gave up trying to find a publisher. Thus when Jo declared her own interest in writing a playback book, I was living with the failure of my own. She wrote *Improvising Real Life* and found a publisher right away. The book appeared in 1993. It was a tense moment for our relationship, and emerging from it without a rupture required our most honest communication and

---

*Another remarkable moment from that gathering: Our daughters had joined a demonstration against the first G.W. Bush presidency, which consisted of a group of women, naked, lying in the snow in New York's Central Park and spelling out with their bodies "No Bush." Jo happened to mention it to the conference attendees. On the last day we were presented with buttons that showed men from the gathering, also naked, also supine, spelling out "No Bush." They had managed a secret photo session the day before in the main hall.

integrity. I recognized her right to express herself and that her book did not compete with mine in what it attempted to do. She recognized the difficulty her success caused me and was instrumental in persuading me to self-publish my book, which eventually appeared in 1994, under our own imprint, Tusitala Publishing, almost a decade after completing the initial draft.

At times I felt that all my efforts, both with the company and on my own, met a wall so solid I could not break through — not in my case a glass ceiling, but perhaps a "fifth wall." It was exhausting and demoralizing.

Termination

The theatre company was once invited to Canada. We drove up in Jo's and my old car. Naturally it broke down on the highway. Under the car, trying to reattach the muffler with the traffic thundering by and my mind full of details for this international mini-tour, I hurt the muscles of my back. Its chronic tightness remains, a reminder of my tendency to shoulder too much. For the actors, this trip to Toronto was little more than an adventure, but for me, it constituted hours and hours of organizing and hope for a new kind of audience. In general, I took too much upon myself (the dark side of Ernest Becker's syndrome). Many were the times I arrived at rehearsals too exhausted from being executive director to be a creative artistic director. Many were the times I walked onto the stage failing to find the needed empty mind for spontaneous performing because my head was stuffed up with administrative worries.

Most importantly, as I grew more and more fatigued, I did not make plans for succession. How could the original company thrive if I were not there to lead it? By 1985 our overall energy and enthusiasm had started to decline. Maintaining our payments to the five actors on contract and our manager was a constant burden. We had our split between those on contract and those not on contract. At the start I had loved the challenge of striving to fill so many different roles — visionary, dramaturg, director, performer, institution-builder. But in the end, it was too much, especially when the goal, presenting a new form of theatre in a familiar, fundable look, proved so elusive.

That year after an elaborate audition process we took on a new actor, and I remember his befuddlement as he slowly learned how tired and dispirited the whole ensemble had become. Looking back, it was a short trajectory—five years of experimentation, five years of achievement, then decline.

In 1986 when I said I was ready to stop, there was no cry to continue without me. It seemed the others were also ready for a change (except perhaps that disillusioned new actor). We closed our office, halted our rehearsal schedule, and used the money in the bank to give ourselves each a silver Playback pin. Then Jo, the kids, and I took off to New Zealand for six months.

Jo remembers the relief of letting go of the struggle. For me relief was mixed with a sense of failure like pepper and salt.

In fact, we did not end abruptly. We reverted to a relaxed state that we had never actually practiced, performing only when an invitation spoke to us, only when we felt like it. We maintained an annual summertime performance for our hometown audience through 1992, when the death of our beloved actor Michael from AIDS brought even these shows to an end.

In time two members of the group started their own playback theatre companies. So from the ashes rose new life: Jo, Hudson River Playback Theatre and Judy, the living room playback sessions (they actually took place in her garage) that eventually became Community Playback Theatre. Both companies still exist. But I never started nor joined a performing company again.

I had tried to bring playback theatre into the mainstream. I did not come close, defeated by a deep official skepticism and by our own internal inconsistencies.

I just went and found that silver pin, long buried in a box. It's beautiful. Made by a local artist, it shows the original playback dancing figures, a Jo Salas design. Almost thirty years have gone by. Maybe I can wear it now.

CHAPTER EIGHT

Reaching for the World

After the original company shut its doors I spent years in limbo.

I taught part-time in the theatre department at the local college and other institutions.

I also taught psychodrama, both as a guest trainer for established training programs and on my own, although the mantle of psychodramatist did not fit any better than did theatre professor.

I took an assortment of other jobs, all related to spontaneous drama. I was hired as a consultant for various schools projects. I was hired to train alcoholism counselors. The young president of an insurance company, just taking over from his father, brought me in, to everyone's puzzlement. My work was a pastiche, and each December, as Christmas neared, I submitted myself to a worried assessment: how much might I earn from where so that we would survive in the coming year.

I wondered if my work with playback was over. However, each time it seemed that it might be out of my life for good, an invitation would come from somewhere.

Even without the original company, playback theatre lived on through the tendrils of interest that had started to snake out from New York State. We were invited to Chicago and were so eager, despite hardly getting paid, that we drove out there, three of us, a day and a night at the wheel (no breakdowns this time). The work is a blur, except for a vivid memory of our host sleeping on a couch in the back of the space as we taught. What message were the students getting from this, I thought? It couldn't be good. Nevertheless we carried on, grateful for a chance to show the work.

The calls were sporadic. I had a devil of a time knowing how to fit this very occasional playback work into my financial projections. But they did keep coming.

I traveled to Texas, where they whisked me from the airport to talk business—as in, how playback could become a successful business—and presented me with custom-made boots (I declined the silver belt buckle). I nodded wisely, remaining silent about our recent income struggles. I traveled to Virginia, Colorado, Oregon, Washington State, and Alaska. We were invited to California, where a student in San Francisco insisted on attending with his parrot. "Robertito comes to all my workshops. He's very well behaved," said the man. Sometimes I coached a blossoming playback theatre company. Most of the time I led a weekend workshop open to all.

Gradually requests also came from overseas: Japan, Germany, Switzerland, France, Sweden, Norway, Italy, New Zealand, Australia, Canada. Often the invitation came from private individuals, and occasionally from an established institution, such as a theatre school, educational development center, drug rehab facility, or corporate training program. Their names had an impressive ring: École de Théâtre de la Ville du Havre, Zentralstelle für Lehrerinnen und Lehrerfortbildung, Centro Italiano di Solidarità don Mario Picchi, and Shakai Sangyo Kyo Iku Kenkyu Jo (Research and Consultation Center for Social Growth, abbreviated as R&C). And yet the requests were very spread out; I did not know where they might come from, or when.

By 1990, recognizing that playback was not falling into oblivion despite the demise of the original company, but even apparently growing, several of us initiated the International Playback Theatre Network (IPTN). The first international conference took place in Sydney two years later. We did not drive the start-up of new groups; it seemed to be happening around us. I was pleased, seeing this activity as a confirmation of our commitment to a kind of open-source philosophy. But I was still slack, still smarting, not fired up. I simply accepted one offer, and then the next.

Some of my American workshops took place in lovely locations, like a ranch in the foothills of the Rocky Mountains, with elk staring at us from the slopes above. But many of them were situated in drab places, even malls — the familiar surrounds of a dispiriting commercialized culture. The European locations, studios located in old buildings on narrow streets, undominated by billboards and flashing signs, tended to be more to my liking. Take me to a studio on a cobbled street in Brescia, or by a lake in Rautalampi.

In fact in many ways my family background primed me to travel the world. As a child with two families and thin roots to any particular neighborhood, I was familiar with the feeling of being a stranger and practiced in cultural navigation. To be abroad was to be a legitimate stranger, a kind of liberation, while being alone in your own land was uncomfortable in a more complex sense.

My family was very international. One grandfather died in Asia on a government mission; the other in Europe where he often went for scholarly work; one grandmother lived her final years in Paris; the other was a German translator. My mother grew up in England, while my father ended up traveling the world for a foundation. And I was by heritage a Jew after all, with wandering in my ancestral past. All this undoubtedly underpinned my formative years away from the United States, especially in Nepal and New Zealand.

Learning the language of my hosts was an added attraction. In speaking French, Nepali, German, Italian, or Japanese, what I longed for was not fluency — I never became truly fluent in anything other than English — but the repeated chance to utilize the language part of my brain. To be conversing in a different phonic palette was a kind of ecstatic music to me, each moment a spontaneity test demanding use of the whole body to compensate for lack of verbal efficiency, not totally unlike improvisational theatre. Even German, which I half expected to shy away from, both because of its reputation as harsh-sounding as well as its role as the language of Hitler, brought me only joy as I started to learn the marvel of its grammar, its fascinating relation to English, and its magnificent sui generis vocabulary.

Wild Boar Beware

I went to Switzerland, where Annette Henne, a woman not afraid to try something new, whether South American mushrooms, New

Mexican yurts, or playback theatre, led a group that practiced in the studio connected to her parents' house. She was also connected to the German psychodrama networks and eventually introduced many Germans to playback. They included Marlies Arping, a founder of playback theatre groups in Cologne and later Frankfurt. Marlies would become the German translator of my book Acts of Service, while Annette would later write a book from her residence in Bali based on some of my statements. Marlies became partners with Daniel Feldhendler, who first came to New York to study playback in 1991. Who was this handsome man, we thought at the time, coming all the way from Europe to learn playback? Daniel, with a background in Theatre of the Oppressed as well as psychodrama, worked as a language professor specializing in dramaturgical approaches. All three started to build interest in Germany for playback and for me as a teacher. Eventually I would find myself going to this part of the world virtually every year.

I was invited to work with a group in Kassel, and a professor of education from that group, Heinrich Dauber, once he verified that *Acts of Service* was a serious work (at least it had an index and bibliography), began to secure invitations from his university, culminating in a guest professorship in 1997 during which we organized a playback theatre symposium.

There were many wonderful moments, both within the workspace and outside it. Heinrich, a man of radical leanings as well as transpersonal sensibilities, was a protégé of Ivan Illich. When I visited he always took me to the nearby Reinhartswald, that ancient forest where the Brothers Grimm set their tales, where amid towering oaks and always on the lookout for wild swine we talked of Paulo Freire, playback, and nondualistic experience.

Once I offered a workshop called "die Regeln von Playback-Theater" (the Rules of Playback Theatre). On the first day we put big sheets of paper on the wall for the purpose of recording the rules as they came up. Some of the participants were both profoundly disappointed and genuinely miffed when on the last day the papers were still untouched. I can't remember exactly how this happened. I didn't plan it, but I was mischievously pleased by the end result.

After these workshop days, we would usually all eat together, meals that could take hours in the relaxed European fashion (good for language learning but sometimes hard on a tired teacher who had to plan for the next day).

Once I started to visit Germany I soon got over a knee-jerk prejudice about the land of the Nazis. After all, most of the people I met there were born after World War II. If anything they were much greater victims than I would ever be. The past was past.

As my relationship with Germany deepened, Heinrich asked me: "Did your family suffer during the War?" He had a particular purpose, since the University of Kassel had a special guest professorship for Jewish scholars whose families had been victims of the Holocaust. "No," I said. Each year he would ask again, and I had to tell him that in fact my Jewish grandfather Elias Lowe, the paleographer who studied Latin manuscripts, got his PhD in Germany and my non-Jewish grandmother H.T. Lowe-Porter was the translator who brought Thomas Mann's work into English. On the contrary, I said, since my family, if anything, only benefited from its connection to German culture, there was no way I would qualify for this post. (The only person in my mostly Jewish immediate family who suffered was my Catholic uncle, Matt, who was caught and sent to Buchenwald for protecting Dutch Jews. My little brother was named after him.)

Heinrich himself felt that the War had dealt a shattering blow to German culture. He wrote in his essay "Songlines," published in the book *Gathering Voices,* which came out of the Kassel symposium: "What would have become of today's Europe, if these [cultural] traditions had not been lost almost two generations ago? And what would have become of America without the influence of the scientists, artists, and authors who fled Europe?"[10]

Much has been written about the extent to which the Germans have come to terms with their country's past. Some inside Germany say that public media is relentless in its reminders, while others would argue that true reflection is just as constantly shirked. In my view, such momentous crimes will take generations to overcome, both for those inside and outside Germany. Especially since I am a Jew, even though nonreligious and not directly touched by the Holocaust, the shadow of Nazism is inescapable. To be in Germany and to think about these things, and to know that most of our countries are guilty of unexpiated crimes, has been instructive. But these thoughts stir unease. And who knows? Perhaps the ghosts of my Jewish ancestors rise up behind my shoulders when I go anywhere near the former Pale of the Settlement (northeastern Europe, where the Jews were confined and from where they often emigrated), whispering, "We fled here for a reason. Go home, go home!"

Raking the Stones

I am lying in the unused study of a corporate trainer with his own very successful company, so successful, in fact, that he rarely comes home. It is a cluttered room, dusty and dark with drawn curtains. A high-end desk is covered with unopened gifts, with more stuff on chairs. A stifling, soulless room. I am sleeping here on the foldout couch. Before I am finished one or two of the unopened items will be offered to me—a state-of-the-art voice recorder, a travel alarm. The boss has made a name for himself by importing humanistic psychology techniques to Japan. He has taken the risk of inviting me to teach playback theatre; the first tryout went well, and starting in 1984, he has invited me back each year for a weekend workshop, a bit of playful relief for his hard-driven customers. We work in hotel conference rooms. The windows are covered there, too. The walls are gray. The floors are dull-colored carpet.

This is Tokyo, a model of modernity, a place where people have the cash to buy things, where hurrying is a way of life, and you see signs of commerce everywhere.

They were in many ways unpleasant, these trips to Japan. But I was getting paid, which for our struggling family meant everything at the time.

There was another side, however. You could sense that underneath the surface lay old and persistent traditions. When the Japanese were not grabbing a bite from an international fast food chain, they were eating at restaurants where the food was amazingly elaborate, as were the manners for eating it. Even in many offices, shoes were removed, and there were layers and layers of customs that people were aware of if not still honoring. Japan remained the home of the real tea ceremony. Of everyday calligraphy.

My workshops were held in Tokyo and Kyoto. Once, touring the ancient temples of Kyoto and appreciating the Zen gardens, so simple, so spare, so profound in their impression, I said wistfully, "This would be a wonderful place to hold a playback workshop." To my surprise, the boss's wife heard me, and for the next and subsequent years our Kyoto training was held in Daishin-In, a very old temple. We worked in the hondo, the temple main hall, a room hundreds of years old with a floor that creaked loudly when you trod on it. The walls were open to a garden where each fallen leaf, each stone, was considered precious. One often looked out and saw someone raking — not a gardener, but the head monk. When it rained, the drops fell off the tiled roof in a poetry of natural sound. We slept there on futons in traditional tatami-floored rooms. The monks served us temple food. The training organization worried at first that the corporate clientele would spurn such simplicity, but in fact they liked it, being reminded, perhaps, of an older, slower time.

Despite the schizophrenic quality of modern Japanese culture, I rejoiced at the chance to glimpse a world that, from reading descriptions of traditional Japanese theatre, had intrigued me from the start. It was so exciting to visit the Noh theatre. There is a stage. There is audience seating. But the feeling of separation is much less than in a Western, proscenium hall. Musicians and scene changers are visible. The atmosphere is not unlike a temple. (If the patron from heaven should ever offer to build me a theatre, I would take as a model Noh theatre design.) In Noh the courtiers and attendants kneel on stage in a posture of humble servitude, and aficionados watch to note how uniformly and effortlessly they rise to their feet when the play calls for it. This uniform rising may seem minor (though after being motionless on one's knees for thirty minutes it is very difficult to do properly), but it creates an effect, which along with other ritual elements captures the audience's ... not attention, but something else ... actually, it doesn't "capture" anything. Rather it helps transport them to another place, one outside their rational thought.

Both the formal aspects of Japanese traditional arts and the old customs lingering in everyday life helped me appreciate the importance of structure to our playback theatre presentation. Improvisation might be our byword. But there was this other aspect, the ritual. The teller came to the chair. The teller told. The actors performed the enactment. With a look, the actors "gave" the story back to the teller. The teller was given the last word. The teller returned to the audience. This sequence, and others that slowly took hold, were rules that demanded adherence (and should, in fact, have been transcribed in my German "Rules" workshop). Like the Japanese custom of leaving your shoes at the door, they offered a sense of propriety and security, and subsequently, what was most important, a feeling of relaxation and freedom.

Tēnā koutou!

Traveling to New Zealand in 1966 changed my life because I met Jo. Traveling there and to Australia in 1980 for our playback tour was another watershed. It brought us an experience of affirmation. At the same time, we received, then and on many subsequent exchanges, learnings that would touch us deeply.

Everyone in New Zealand knows about Te Rauparaha, the Maori warrior. Two centuries ago he mounted his sorties from Kapiti Island, off the west coast of the North Island. Today Kapiti is a nature sanctuary, famous for its birds, including the hard-to-spot kiwis. Bev Hosking introduced us to a community hall in sight of Kapiti in a tiny town called Paekakariki. The floor is wood. The windows are large. The space is big enough for running games. If you hold your breath for a moment, you can hear the sound of the sea, just across the road.

When we have done trainings there, everyone stays in the motor camp a few blocks away on simple bunks. We all share in the cooking. It is in the frontier, down-home, do-it-yourself tradition of this small island country. Our work together and the stories we share meld with the delicious smell of toast, the joy of playing games on the grass, and the splendid view across the water.

Most of the workshops I have joined in this place have started in a ceremonial way, with a Maori playbacker, Christian Penny, conducting a simple version of the welcome in Maori known as a powhiri. He would also express Maori words of thanks at the gathering's end. Christian spoke in a strong voice, full of passion, almost fierce. I was always impressed. What a contrast to the typically ragged start of a workshop in America, where either the leader talks or there is a go-around of names. Here we would also have the leader talk, also have a go-around of names. But something had to come first. The welcome. The host person said it to the guest. At the end, the guest said a last word and turned to the host, who took back the authority of the gathering and pronounced the final words. Here was living ritual. It suited an oral form like playback theatre.[11]

So did the hospitality code of the New Zealanders and the Australians. In a city-based workshop, if any participants came from other towns, the locals would put them up. No one would be expected to pay for a hotel. This looking out for each other also appealed to me greatly.

One of the sponsors of our first trip Down Under was a theatre school in Sydney called the Drama Action Centre. It was run by a couple, Francis Batten and Bridget Brandon, and taught clown work and commedia dell'arte. It also had an applied theatre focus. Even more important, Francis and Bridget had studied Morenean methods. They and a number of their students would go on to become playback theatre company directors and teachers, including Mary Good of Melbourne, Bev Hosking of Wellington, and Martin and Marilyn Sutcliffe of Auckland. They would make a significant artistic contribution, introducing new forms later adopted by playback theatre companies far and wide (such as tableau stories and chorus).

They also understood about the value of open, honest interpersonal communication. They sought, as we did, a balance between artistic work and true dialogue, and they aspired to a refreshing level of ethical practice, both on stage and in life. Mary and Bev would in time become leaders of the world playback network, the IPTN.

When we first started our own training courses, soon after that first trip to the southern world, we followed our new colleagues' example, putting up students at our house and arranging for their stay with friends and neighbors. We all made food together. We picked up students at the station beforehand and then drove them back to the station when it was all over. I remember one student for a psychodrama workshop who told me later how uncomfortable she had been to stay at the house of the trainer (maybe a factor was psychodrama's alliance with the culture of psychotherapy, which discouraged personal contact between client/student and therapist/teacher). Such feedback did not change our ways. We prized community outside of the work as well as inside it, even though for us as organizers, it took much extra effort. The payoff was a sense of shared adventure and a deeper personal encounter. Only the later growth of our programs forced us to give up this hospitable "down under" approach; what was feasible with seven visitors became overwhelming with eighteen and totally impossible with a hundred.

Comfort Women

Knowing that I perform and teach in many places around the globe, people often ask me, "Are the stories very different from culture to culture?"

Traveling has taught me that human love and longing is fundamentally similar everywhere, no matter how unfamiliar and strange people may seem through the filter of one's own culture and experience. I began to learn this lesson on my verandah in Nepal.

During my second or third visit to Australia the workshop participants revolted after two or three days of hearing me as conductor send the story to the actors with a dramatic "Watch!"

"It sounds so rude!" they said.

"How should I do it?" I asked, genuinely puzzled.

"*Let's* watch," they suggested, a softer command. Since then, bowing to internationalism, I have abandoned my gruff New York City "Watch!" for "Let's watch."

The Japanese parent who tells a worried story about her depressed adult son (see Yorimi's story in the Workshop chapter) is no different from parents everywhere who will never cease worrying for their children, but this story also reveals aspects of youthful alienation characteristic of modern Japan. The Lithuanian who tells a story of being stopped at the border crossing into Austria is touching on universal fears facing travelers at frontiers; yet knowledge of Central European history and culture will bring out an extra edge to the tale.

There is similitude between the world of a cultural group and that of a community group. Each community has its own history and social mores. As does a family. As does, in fact, each individual. While at bottom we are all part of the human family, we come, paradoxically, from our own infinitely different personal and communal worlds. Finding the commonality while elucidating what is different, what is unique, is part of our task as playback theatre performers. It is one of the reasons I wanted my actors in the original company to carry notebooks—always to be a student of the groups they encountered, always to be recording new information. Our stories have resonances often elusive to outsiders.

An example, from a Japanese woman teller, who is a schoolteacher:

> *I decided to go to Korea on holiday, just to learn about the country. On the plane it was so strange—I noticed that I was just about the only woman. Then after one day in Seoul I happened to pass one of the men from the plane walking with a young Korean woman. I didn't know what to make of it, and when I got home and mentioned it in the teachers', room, one of my colleagues, a man, said matter-of-factly, "It's sexual tourism. I've done it myself."*

Depending on the status of women in one's own culture, this story carries a horrifying punch. But its full dimension is hard to comprehend without knowledge of the Japanese conquest of Korea in World War II and the forced labor of the Korean "comfort women" servicing Japanese soldiers. This story suggests that an unacknowledged or not fully acknowledged past oppression will live on, if in a somewhat altered form.[12]

Another instance, this time from a Frenchman:

81

I was one of the ones who couldn't keep a tune. In elementary school, the teacher always told me to be quiet when the others were singing.

A very short story, apparently without much to it, but widely recognizable. It seems that music teachers often try to shush pupils who are less musical. But to enact this story merely on a psychological level does not do it justice, despite its brevity. If we unpack some of the background, we begin to get a larger picture. I sensed the teller was Jewish. Since he was middle-aged, I knew he would have been in elementary school around 1950, just after World War II. At home he might have been learning of the decimation of his extended family. I could imagine that the climate in that classroom was not friendly to a Jewish boy.

Can we wonder that he couldn't find the note to express himself in music class, to lift his voice in joyful song? Can we not understand when, forty-odd years later, as a teller he still cannot easily find the words to flesh out his story? As his conductor I imagined some of these resonances, but did not know how to voice them. So I simply sent the bare story to the actors, who in their turn could not find the deeper meaning and produced an enactment without much flair.

Despite differences of culture and the frequent muffling of the past by the present, individuals far apart, from Trondheim to Turin, Curitiba to Kiev, raised their hands to tell their story.

Sometimes the stories emerge almost with a sense of secrets revealed. They confront an ever-present tension between a need for revelation and a need for the protective veil of silence. These kinds of stories may have universal themes, but the specific content is unique to each context. Can we imagine sexual tourism in contemporary Korea? Can we imagine life for a Jewish schoolboy in postwar France?

So many life-changing stories flood my memory, both cautionary, shattering, and inspiring: the Japanese man who recounted that when his wife was giving birth to their first child, he was drunk in another part of town; the teller from Northern Ireland, who after seeing her story enacted could not stop crying; the African-American man who said that the Fourth of July holiday was not *his* Independence Day; the escaped Argentinian dissident who never saw her mother again; the Austrian voicing with pride his decades-long secret Jewish name.

Listening to tellers from around the world has built a sense of common humanity, but even more it has also been a vivid education about stories belonging to a specific time and place beyond my knowledge or experience.

Chapter Nine

School I

"Happy birthday to you! Happy birthday to you!"

So many beaming faces, flushed with love (love?) for their teacher. I am the teacher, and we are at a famous American growth center near New York City. We are one of dozens of weekend personal development workshops on offer. The center's interest in playback had seemed an opportunity, and I hadn't considered the date when scheduling the gig. Now that I was here, I realized my mistake. On this birthday I wanted to be home with the kids, not introducing fluid sculptures to a dozen newbies. I had kept my birthday a glum secret, but the word had got out, and first my class, then groups of people I didn't know at all, were circling me and singing the birthday song. What an agony!

Indeed there was a superficiality to these growth center classes that made me uneasy. The participants were mostly "tasting," and they exuded a New Age positivism that in my view ignored structural injustices in the United States and elsewhere. In time we would be invited by many such places, then dropped. Ultimately we and the growth centers turned out not to be a good fit. One problem, I think, was that what we were offering, which attracted 15 rather than 50 or 150 students, did not pull in enough enrollment income.

I remember my dismay one year when I showed up for our workshop at one of these places, whose brochures ooze respect and empathy, to find we had been assigned to work in a living room full of couches. It felt like a deliberate insult, since it was not our first time there; they certainly knew we needed space for dancing and movement. What was behind such an egregious mistake, I wondered? Why invite us if we were not truly welcome?

For many years I approached these short, introductory work-shops in a spirit of having to prove something. I used all my energy to enthuse and impart. But how far, in fact, could one get in a weekend? One could teach this form or that, but in so short a time to get the essence of playback experience across was an uncertain proposition. It was just too short and depended on too many contextual elements, such as the size of the group and how many couches were cluttering up the room.

On my annual trips to Japan for R&C I eventually abandoned my effort to "teach playback" and accepted my task of providing a fun, engaging personal development workshop. To be sure, I always taught at least one playback form, sometimes two, and I always would do at least one full playback story. But beyond that, I would see who was there and what activities inspired me. Over time, the superficiality of this work was not sustaining. It was nice to be the guest guru. I might have built it into a career and developed a format that would appeal to a crowd, traveling the world with my "workshop" and selling pricey "product." ("Always have your product on display at the back of the room," one expert told me.)

But ultimately, such a role was not me. In fact, I yearned for the opposite—to go deeper into the richness of the playback method, to make new discoveries with it, to have more time with the students, and to have more commitment from them as well. (Despite the brevity of my Japan workshops, some of the students would feel the same way and urge me to reorganize my work there.)

The year I had to take that full-time college teaching job my father, in order to buck me up, said, "You're a natural teacher." But rather than console me, his remark plunged me into gloom. To me, taking that job only rubbed salt in the wound of my failure to make the theatre company sustainable. The fact is, however, that although I could not at the time admit it to myself, my identity was already undergoing a shift. More than circumstance was pushing me toward teaching.

Performing playback theatre was exciting, but it also had its drawbacks. The main one was time. In the two-hour framework of the modern theatre show, we were always battling the ice of a cold, reserved audience or the fire of one that was overheated. In one, tellers hesitated to raise their hand. In the other, many hands flew up at once. Many shows had ended on an unsatisfying note because as conductor I had not been able to negotiate creatively the raft of hands demanding to be chosen for the last story.

The workshop setting, on the other hand, benefited from an extended time frame. There was still the challenge of the improvisational moment. There was still performance (although not so high-pressure). But there were also discussion, deep exercises, and time between sessions for informal contact.

I found I liked more and more this stretched-out rhythm, especially when instead of one day or two days (the growth center model) we had five days, or even more. I could get to know the students as persons; they could get to know me. I found each personal conversation, impossible in the performance context, precious. And most of the time, the work went deeper, for the simple reason that there was more time to build group trust, to let the iron bars of protection open, to find one's truth.

What enriched me most were people's stories, and more stories came out over the workshop period. A thicker, deeper web was woven. To my surprise I found as the years passed I was not dreaming of starting another performing company. And I slowly came to accept my father's words. I liked teaching workshops—if we could really go on a journey together. If we were not afraid of the big stories. If we were committed to learning what was necessary to dramatize them. If we had the strength and courage to undertake a rite of passage, after which we might not be the same ever again.

Jerzy Grotowski abandoned performance in 1975 for what he called "paratheatrics." In the United States, Anna Halpern and Ruth Zaporah, among others, shifted toward healing rituals and transpersonal explorations. Like them, I seemed to be moving from an outlook dominated by theatre performance to one "beyond theatre."

It was a very big shift of identity. However, while the event might be termed a workshop instead of a performance and while the participants might be termed students rather than spectators, the core of the work remained the same: a performative moment enacting personal narrative.

Clearly those intro workshops and "tasters" tended to be less than ideal, including putting me in the position of continually waiting for invitations. Could I set up something meatier, I wondered? Something with more substance? With a sequence that went from the beginner to advanced level? An actual school?

Screams from Within

From the early 1980s on we offered short summer trainings, attended by students at all levels. The most dramatic moment of this early period was the arrival of five members of a playback theatre group in Russia. How they got there was a kind of miracle with a too-long story behind it. But when they walked in, especially for us Americans present, who had been fed anti-Soviet stories since we were tiny, it was an exhilarating moment, representing the power of ordinary people to come together through passion and creativity. Only one of them spoke English. Fortunately one spoke some French, another some German. So we got by. But on that occasion we were thrilled just to be together. The Russians had much to learn about playback — after all, their founder had only seen one performance on a visit to the Netherlands — but they brought with them in exchange a background in Russian stagework that was exciting to behold.

On that occasion I phoned the chairman of the college's theatre department where I had taught as an adjunct. He was not in, but on his voicemail I told him excitedly about the Russians.

"It's fantastic," I said. "Russian acting on our doorstep. You might want to invite them to visit."

He never phoned back, and then they were gone. Was his outlook just too provincial to appreciate visitors imbued with the tradition of Stanislavsky and Meyerhold, Kandinsky and Stravinsky? Did he dismiss them because playback theatre left him cold (he was a die-hard theatre theatre man). Was he so overworked that any extra task was just too much? Probably a mix of all these things. But to totally ignore this cultural gift! I was astounded.

Jo and I had some sense of the personal richness of the Russian artistic tradition when after a two-person summer playback performance for Jewish retirees in upstate New York some years earlier, we had been introduced to a Russian émigré actor named Aleksandr Benyaminov. Our whole family had subsequently visited his flat in the Bronx, where I saw posters of his many productions in Leningrad on the wall. What had impressed me most, however, were his paintings and sculptures, which he had made as part of his preparation for stage roles. These works said to me that he had benefited from rehearsal periods generous enough to support such full studies. His flat was like a miniature museum, and it left me full of respect.

Aleksandr had paid us one of our greatest compliments after that summertime show. With a hand pointing downward, he had moved his second and third fingers on the table to show a person walking. In his minimal English, he said, as his fingers walked, "Marcel Marceau — always the same. But you — deep."

The decision to expand our trainings had not come easy, for although tired of the stand-alone workshop routine, I feared the failure that might come from a more ambitious program. Unlike theatre schools located in big cities, we could not support a full-time set-up. Originally I conceived of only four-day courses because I could not imagine students committing to more, but my friend René the psychodramatist urged me to follow my conviction rather than be driven by expediency.

So I summoned my courage. We would offer a summer program. The courses would be progressive. They would follow a "spiral" pedagogical model — each level offered basically the same curriculum — acting, conducting, music, narrative theory, company life, social awareness, applications, ethics — but at a more sophisticated level. Each stage demanded more from the student: two-day courses became five days became ten days became three weeks. Before entering the advanced level students had to complete independent study projects at home. At the end they received a diploma.

As a site we chose a fixed-up barn converted into an arts center called Unison, surrounded by hayfields and trees — ashes, oaks, maples, familiar to me since childhood — home to barred owls and bobolinks, raccoons and squirrels and deer. To get there you turned off the asphalt road and went a short ways along dirt bordered by wildflowers. It was a simple structure, one big room with a wide-planked floor, with performance seating for fifty at most. Off the main space was a small kitchen. When we needed a breakout room we used the outdoors. There was no overnight accommodation, but we were not put off. Some of the students camped in the field. Others we put up with friends. Some stayed in motels in town, only three kilometers away. "No bus?" asked a German student, used to civic amenities. "No bus," we replied, and although the distance was not far, walking along the narrow-shouldered county road was neither safe nor pleasant. So once arrived at this little community arts center, you tended to stay put, especially if you did not have your own car.

As with our decision not to control or franchise the playback method, here also I insisted that the diploma would have meaning only if the school's reputation merited it. There would be no attempt to certify or license graduates. Any playback theatre practitioner could choose to attend or not. It would be up to us to make the program worthwhile.

As I ordered stationery and prepared a letter advertising the first year's program, I realized that I was letting go of any thought of leaving playback theatre. I had dropped it, and now it was pulling me back, enticing me to commit myself once again.

But this time would be different, I vowed. I would not get trapped in a struggling nonprofit. I would not hold onto a dream of grant support. In fact, I would proudly set up my own business. In my mind I thought I might even make some money. Why not? Didn't I deserve it? The new institution would be called the Jonathan Fox School of Playback Theatre. The title was a nod to the idea of humility (after all, there might eventually be many other schools of playback theatre; mine would be just one of them), but the opposite sense also rang true. I had had enough of collaboration and was ready to stand on my own feet. Why not call it by my own name?

The names of the four courses we offered that first summer in

1993 were PT Basics, Games, Songs, and Warm-ups, Communication and Change, and the ten-day First-Year Intensive (later called Playback Theatre Practice). Undermining my independent-mindedness right from the start, I asked Jo to co-teach two of them with me.

We had many vivid moments in that old barn.

On the second day of one workshop, we invited the group of about twelve students to do some social mapping: Who is part of a PT company? How many years have you been involved in PT? We asked people to place themselves in a line or location according to their answers. A couple of the questions were social in nature: Who works together? Who is a couple? At this last question, a handsome man from Europe and an even handsomer woman from the US looked meaningfully at each other, then they both stepped into the circle with a smile. They had never met before the class, but we had put them both up in Judy's (refurbished) garage. Evidently they had gotten to know one another overnight.

A reporter came to write an article about the Jonathan Fox School. It was mid-morning. As I stood outside, explaining, as one often had to: "No, it is not therapy. We are offering theatre training," a spine-chilling scream came from inside. "It sounds like primal therapy!" said the reporter, looking nervous. "No, no," I said. The scream came again. "Nothing like that." An even louder scream. "Our students come from all over," I said lamely, trying to divert her attention. She did not stay long.

Establishing the School was a gesture of acceptance of my place in the growing playback theatre movement. It would hopefully ensure a regular income for our family (at ages forty-four and fifty, Jo and I finally aspired to buy a house) and enable me to escape the guru circuit. Most of all, I looked forward to more chance to exercise my calling as an animator of everyday actors.

The three-week PT Leadership class was the acme of my teaching, and from 1994 to 2010, when I started to cede way to others, I was its only faculty. Three weeks provided so many juicy learning moments and heart-thumping challenges. We had time to create a deep group sense and take big risks. As the teacher I often felt stretched to the fullest (which was one of the pedagogical purposes for having a long residential class—so that the students could see the teacher stumble). The day-to-day intensity and demand for concentration was so great that by the class's end I could hardly move for exhaustion. But I loved it.

At our graduation ceremony, Jo, other colleagues, and I always performed for the students, and each graduate was invited to make a personal statement. Their words of reflection on their playback journey were often moving. I gave a tiny talk, too, each time trying to find the right story to fit the occasion. Sometimes I used a toy animal as a co-speaker. A favorite in later years was a wooden camel called Mahfouz (the name inspired by the Egyptian Nobel Prize laureate, Naguib Mahfouz). To each of my homilies (exhorting the students to make good use of what they learned, urging them to use playback for the community benefit), Mahfouz would pour his scorn. He was in such contrast to us, who strove constantly to be earnest, polite, and considerate with each other.

"I'm saying my truth, Mahfouz!" I would plead. "To the students! Please don't cut me off." Laughter.

"I spit on your truth. I spit on your students!" More laughter.

These little ceremonies traditionally ended with champagne and roses—and joyful celebration.

CHAPTER TEN

Workshop

The venue is called Falling Waters, a retreat center for Dominican nuns.* Located on spacious grounds bordering the majestic Hudson River of New York State, it is a stunning spot in summer. Even in winter, however, when the house is available for rental to people like us, the view out across the ice-chocked river is exciting. Inside it is cozy, with a large living room area we strip of furniture to serve as a workspace, and a single room for each student, spare but comfortable. The two elderly nuns, Sister Catherine and Sister Peggy, who prepare the food and run the house, embody good cheer and unstinting service.

As I drive up to begin the four-day workshop, I am thinking of business matters. There will be seven students, a disappointing number, just adequate in terms of the work but under par in terms of making any income, especially since three of them are on scholarship. The low enrollment puts me in a bad mood.

After greeting the sisters and giving them some Valentine's Day chocolate, which I know they like, I head for the workspace. I am a good hour early. I see a lithe young man, very short-haired, with a scarf around his neck. It is Francis from San Diego. He greets me with a beautiful smile. He is skinny as a rail. "We'll start at two in the main room," I tell him.

---

*Failing to write up a specific workshop in a way that worked on the page, I was able to give a sense of the experience by amalgamation. The description in this account is therefore a composite, with invented names (although the names of the venue itself and the nuns who worked there are real). The performance of the original company described in Chapter Six uses the real names of its members, but is the result of a similar process of distillation.

As I walk into the dining room, I can see out across the Hudson River, where a barge is being pushed upriver by a tugboat. Two people are in conversation. I introduce myself. One is a middle-aged professor of English named John Simpson. He is a large man and is wearing cowboy boots. The other, also of middle years, is half his size. She tells me her name is Rain Weinstein. She is wearing magenta shoes, a scarf of many colors, and bright red lipstick.

"I'm so excited to be here!" she exclaims.

"I was just speaking about my current project," John tells me in a resonant voice. "A research study that uses playback."

"Really?" I answer.

"We're assessing the efficacy of PT to increase motivation for reading," he said. "We've got a grant from the Oklahoma Arts Council for a three-year..."

I cut him off. "I'm eager to hear about it," I say. "But I have to get ready now. Two o'clock start," I add as I leave them.

This is always an awkward moment for me, the uneasiness of the threshold. Meanwhile I am taking in first impressions. I have introduced myself to Sally Caruthers, a pleasant-looking woman of about fifty who runs a PT group in Connecticut. The only one I am really drawn to is Francis, who seems gentle and maybe creative. I greet Yorimi Yamamoto, Angel Dabboura, and Barbara Alford as they enter the workspace.

"Welcome to this four-day playback theatre conducting workshop," I say, as we begin. "I will say a word about our work plan in a moment. But first let us introduce ourselves." I want them to have the first words. We go around the circle.

"My name is Rain, like what falls on flowers in the spring, and I'm here because I love playback theatre."

"I'm Barbara Alford, from Canada. I work in a clinic, and belong to a playback group in Toronto. I'm here because I wanted to come to the source, to make sure we're doing it right." Her face is reserved.

"My name is Sally Caruthers, from Connecticut." Her bracelets jingle as she talks. "I started a group in my home town in Torrington, Connecticut. We are associated with the town library. I want to pick up ideas for a festival we're having next summer."

"I'm John Simpson. I'm a professor of literature at Babington College in Oklahoma. We're currently engaged on a research study to assess playback's utility in increasing motivation for reading. It's now halfway through. The initial indicators are quite positive..."

I interrupt, aware that I cut him off earlier, but I want to encourage brief statements—a balance of words and silence. "And what is your reason for coming, John?" I ask.

"My reason for coming?" he repeats. "Well, I was introduced to playback by a friend in our town who has a playback group there, and I've been going to rehearsals once in a while. But it seemed since I was directing this study if I got some hands-on experience it might help in making adjustments to the design."

"Thank you, John," I say. "Next?"

"My name is Francis, but my friends call me Spider." He laughs. "It's a long story. Call me whatever, either Francis or Spider. I don't know why I'm here," he says, laughing again. He brushes his hand over his forehead. "Maybe I'm looking for a new direction."

"I am Angel," says the next. She is a striking young black woman with a lilting voice. "From the country of Trinidad and Tobago. But I am studying here at the moment, getting a masters in adolescent studies. I was introduced to playback theatre at UWI and this is my chance to learn more about it. I think it may be very useful for working with young people."

"UWI?" asks Francis.

"University of the West Indies. It is our university at home," Angel says.

I look at the last person. She has Asian features and is sitting very straight with an open notebook in her lap.

"My name is Yamamoto, Yorimi. I am from Japan. I cannot speak English well," she says, with a bow of her head.

I notice that her English is quite good. "Why are you here?"

"A friend suggested I enroll," she says. "I have taken one class of playback theatre in Japan with Yoshihara-sensei. I am visiting America. This class fit my schedule."

The round is finished. It is an inexperienced crew, and I feel a touch of frustration. Wasn't the whole point of the School attracting more advanced practitioners? But I am already starting to be curious about these students, whoever they are.

They are expecting me now to present the curriculum. But I outfox them. "Let's stand up and push the chairs back. You won't need your notebooks," I say.

I put on a lively song. For the next ten to fifteen minutes we engage in physical warm-ups. Silly, easy. Expressive. As we go I invite them to learn the name of their partner, their neighbor, their opposite. I note that a number of our group are quite held in— John, Sally, Yorimi. Francis, on the other hand, moves fluidly. I ask them to pair up (one group of three because of the odd number). We do a mirror exercise. I encourage them to use voice as well as movement. When the action is done, I invite them to share briefly with their partner. It is a first of many exercises in pairs that will help them build connections with each other.

Music, movement, sounds but no words. Connecting, interacting. Then when it is over, words.

Next we do some social mapping. I am hoping this process will ease the students' worry about their vulnerabilities. "Since this is a conducting workshop," I say, "Let's show how much experience we have with conducting—in a line, from the least to the most." The students have to talk to each other to see where they fit. Sally is the most experienced, conducting regularly in her local theatre company.

There is a pair at the other end consisting of Yorimi and Francis. "None!" they say. Angel, John, and Rain explain their limited experience. Barbara says she is not the main conductor in her company, but she conducts in rehearsals.

"How about acting?" I ask. We go through the same process, but this time John is at the inexperienced extreme.

"I'm not afraid," he says, 'but I haven't done it."

Francis heads uncertainly toward the other end of the line. "I'm a dancer," he says, but I don't know much about acting."

"Playback involves a lot of movement. Your dance background will be very useful," I assure him.

Yorimi says, "I think I should watch. My English is not good enough for the acting. Perhaps with conducting, as well."

"We often use minimal language," I answer. "And it often

works to speak in your own language. After all, we have all already heard the story." But there is another issue here—the others' tolerance. So I say to them, "Do you think she should just observe?" "No!" they all reply. "But it means our being very clear with our own language and avoiding some American slang in order to support Yorimi." They nod in acceptance.

I raise another question. "We have two generations here, or almost. How do you feel about that? Let's stand in two islands, the oldies and the youngsters," I say.

They hesitate. There are a couple of giggles. Then they move. Angel, Yorimi, and Francis in one group, John, Sally, Rain, and Barbara in the other.

"How does it feel standing where you are?" I ask.

"I like being around old people," Angel says. There is embarrassed laughter.

"We're not that old!" says Sally.

"It reminds me I have a bad shoulder," says Rain. "I'm worried about aggravating it."

"Age brings wisdom," says John.

"Not always," says Francis from the other side. Laughter again.

"The generations have a lot to share with each other," I say. "But often difference is a source of conflict. We will have to work it out together. I believe that if we find a way to accept and accommodate each other, then we will learn lots together."

"There is one more question," I add. This is the one I have been building toward. It is a map of where they come from. My intention, or rather my hope, is that it will permit the subject of race to emerge in a natural, if indirect, way. I give them the instruction. They position themselves according to an imaginary map of the US in the room, with our venue, Falling Waters, in the center. Sally (Connecticut) stands close to it. Then comes Rain (New York City). Barbara (Toronto) is at one end of the room. Francis (California) stands at another edge. I look for Yorimi.

"Here!" she says, laughing, from the hallway. Angel wanders to one spot, then moves again and puts herself in a southeasterly corner, John to the southwest.

"How does it feel standing where you are?" I ask them.

"I'm not used to winter," says Francis. "I'm used to sun," he says.

"I am a proud westerner," says John, standing tall. Rain says she feels like a citizen of the world, because she has traveled a lot, but also because New York is so multicultural. I call to Yorimi, urging her to come (symbolically as well as literally) at least into the room.

"You have come a long way," I say.

"Yes," she says. "I am looking for the bottom of my rainbow." Her quaint, slightly poetic turn of phrase catches people's attention.

"You started in one place," I say to Angel, the Trinidadian, "then you changed your spot."

"I'm studying in Boston," she says. " I'm living there now. But of course Trinidad is my home. My family is there. So I'm standing in Trinidad."

"How does it feel, standing in Trinidad?"

"I miss home. I miss my culture."

"What's one big difference between there and here?" I ask.

"Everyone here is white!" she says.

"Yes," I respond, "including the teacher" (referring to myself). Taking the opening, I say to her and to the others: "I am a white, male teacher. My position may carry echoes of an old, uncomfortable, traditional authority, although I will do my best not to replicate those patterns." I am glad to get power dynamics named. Angel nods, looking at me full in the face for the first time.

The social mapping phase is over. The hope, of course, is that mentioning these issues now will make it more possible to bring them up later, if they arise in the work. Another purpose is letting individuals know that their own point of worry or isolation is nameable and faceable.

Now I speak about the curriculum. "We will do exercises in conducting, both for beginners and nonbeginners. We will perform together. And we will act out each others' stories." I don't say much beyond that, for as the leader my objective at this point, so close to the start, is to take them away from their accustomed critical thought habits. The thinking and discussion can come later.

The social mapping has meant a lot of talking and standing. It is time for a break. "Eleven minutes!" I announce.

They look up, with curious smiles on their faces. Yorimi looks at her watch, figuring out exactly when eleven minutes will be over.

At the break I go up to John. I feel it is important that I make a good connection with him. "Your project sounds great," I say. "I am sure this process can help students want to read. Acting can prepare them for thinking." I say. "And then there is the work with stories. Making them come alive."

He nods at me. Now is time for our first stories and time to initiate the work they have come for—playback theatre. I sit on the conductor's chair looking at them. First I invite actors to come to the stage area. Francis, Barbara, and Angel come. I praise their courage. They sit on cubes, facing us, expectant. I ask for a musician. Rain comes and sits stage left behind the instruments.

Then I nod to the empty chair next to me. "The teller's chair," I say. "A chair of truth." I pause. "Who wants to tell the first story of our time together?" John quickly raises his hand. I am not surprised. He seems to have a need to be seen. As I say to him, "Come," I store his eagerness in the back of my mind. It may become an issue later.

"Where does your story take place?" I ask him. He plants his feet firmly on the floor.

"In my classroom!" he says.

"Is this story about your project?" I ask at once.

"It sure is," he replies. "I want to tell about how the testing phase is confirming my hypothesis about reading motivation."

"Sure." I say, even though I am not so sure. "Who is important besides you?"

John responds as if he has not heard my question: "We are in a rural area, where many of the kids are not readers. They don't read books. When they get to me they have a resistance to good literature."

"Is that what you want to tell about?" I ask. "The reluctance of your students to read good books?"

"No, this is just part of the background." At the same time, I sense something unclear about his story; it is too abstract. I notice his cowboy boots of brown inlaid leather. "Nice boots you have there," I comment.

He looks at me and smiles. "The best," he says. "You come from rodeo country," I say. I am winging it now.

"I do," he says. "Born and bred." There is a pause. "Actually," he goes on. "Running this experiment feels a little like being in the rodeo. Riding a bronco, you know?" He has shifted. The story is emerging now.

"Tell us about it," I say.

"Most of the time my students are uninterested, laid back, lethargic. The last thing they want to read is Thomas Hardy. But once I get them into action, I can't hold them back. The energy is fantastic. I don't know how to handle it."

"Right!" I say. We almost have all we need for action. "Is it hard to get them going?"

"It's tricky," he answers. "They are reluctant at first. Even with the warm-ups I learned, they hesitate. Then all of a sudden, they're off. It feels explosive. Then I don't know how to rein them in."

"Pick someone to play you," I say, looking at the actors sitting on the cubes. He chooses Barbara. She stands, as all playback actors do when chosen. "What is a word that describes you in this story?" I ask.

John laughs: "Holding on for dear life!" he says.

"Right. The other actors can play your horse, or the students in the class." They stand.

"Do you want me to explain more?" he asks.

"I think we have enough." I say. "OK?"

"OK," he replies.

I give a launching phrase: "We'll now see John's story of the Thomas Hardy rodeo. Let's watch!"

Rain, the musician, plays. The actors take positions. Barbara starts off the scene with a explanation about doing something different. The students are slumped over, hardly listening. She starts to prop them up physically. "Just try this," she urges, moving their bodies. "And this." They are heavy, with drooping heads. She sighs. "And this," she tries once more.

Suddenly the two actors jump up, voices loud, gesticulating, laughing, calling out.

"Whoa!" says the teller's actor. "Steady there!"

"This is fun!" cry the students.

"Steady!" says the professor.

"Cool!" shout the students. By now they have jumped into motion, both of them gyrating and gesticulating. The musician hits a bell.

"Time is up," says the prof.

The students continue. "This is great!" say the students.

"Time!"

"More!"

"We need to end with a discussion. I have questions for you!" says the teacher.

"Got to go!" says one of the students, suddenly cutting the action and heading offstage. "Me, too," says the other.

The teacher looks around his suddenly empty classroom. He sighs. "That was good," he says to himself in monologue in an overwhelmed tone.

Barbara, the actor, ends the scene and looks over at the teller and me.

"Good!" I say. "Great!" It was, I think, a surprisingly successful enactment for a team that does not know each other. They had a sense of the story, and both Angel and Francis moved with energy and grace. "I know it did not focus on the details," I say to John. "But did it capture some of the feeling of your experience?"

John looks at me. "Yes," he says, his voice softer than at the start. "It really does feel that way."

"Thank you, John." He goes back to the audience.

I see that Sally has her hand halfway up, ready to be the teller. "Please come," I tell her.

As she sits, her face is already getting flushed with emotion. "It's about my mother," she says. I know at once this will be a very different kind of interview than the one with John.

"Pick someone to be your mother," I say.[13] She picks Francis. He stands slowly. "A couple of words to describe your mother," I ask.

She sighs, and wipes her eyes with a handkerchief. "Weak and wild."

I look at her and repeat her surprising phrase: "Weak and wild?"

"My mother is seventy-nine. She is very thin. With thin bones. She has MCI, mild cognitive impairment. It's like early Alzheimer's. So sometimes she is confused. But sometimes she is also angry in a way she never was before. She was always the peacemaker in the family. But now... The doctor says she is losing those brain cells that inhibit aggressive action."

I ask: "Do you have in mind a moment when she was this way?"

She is in the flow of her story and doesn't answer my question. "I was worried about coming to this workshop, because I wouldn't be able to check on her for a week."

"Pick a moment," I repeat.

"OK. It was last week. I was visiting her in her retirement home."

I interrupt: "Who can play you?" "Barbara," she says.

"Good. Continue," I say.

"She was complaining about the cold. I went to put a blanket around her."

"Can you tell us just a bit about her room?"

"Oh, it's very nice. But just one room. She has a bed. And a nice chair, where she sits all day, looking out the window. There's the TV, and her dresser. And a big poster with family photos on it."

"Is she sitting in her chair?"

"Yes. I reach over to tuck in the blanket. And suddenly she is furious. She starts yelling, 'Get away! Get away!' And she picks up a glass paperweight and throws it at me. It lands on the floor with a terrible noise. She is yelling. She is hitting me. I am shocked. I'm afraid she is going to hurt herself. She could break a wrist." Sally's voice shows considerable distress.

"How does the scene end?" I ask.

"The aide comes in with her pills, and she is suddenly her sweet self again. I am shaken, but I try not to show it. I say good-bye as usual." She wipes her eyes again.

I give her an empathic look. "We will now see your story," I say, raising my voice a little. "A violent visit. Let's watch!"

Again the musician plays while the actors use cubes and cloth to make a room. This time it does not go quite so smoothly. Francis finds it hard to show an old person's easy chair with just a wooden cube. They use a piece of cloth as the paperweight, and it looks silly as it floats to the floor. But there is still power to the scene, as the mother starts abruptly to shout at her daughter. They tussle with each other. Angel enters as the aide, and the mood abruptly changes. "Sweetie!" greets the mother to the aide. "Hello, darlin'. I've got your pill," says the aide with affection. The aide leaves. The scene ends with Sally the daughter saying weakly, "Goodbye, mother. It was a lovely visit." The actors stand in place, regarding the teller.

"It's so hard," Sally says weeping.

"I can imagine," I say. It seems she does not want to speak more. "Thank you," I say, and she returns to the audience.

"Thank you actors!" I exclaim, as they leave the stage. "And musician." It is almost time for dinner. There is lots to talk about. But I don't want talking. I am happy for people to feel their feelings, whatever they are. As I announce a break, I see Rain approach Sally and give her a long hug.

Bad Cop, Bad Cop

The planning for day two I completed after breakfast before leaving home. It doesn't take me long. We will do some acting review. Then focus on conducting in exercises and stories. It is a brisk day, cold enough to keep the snow from melting. As I enter the building at Falling Waters I review possible start-up activities in my mind, but do not choose one. I'll wait to get inside before I do, so I can gauge the atmosphere. Gone is my ambivalence from the day before. Today I look forward to meeting the students and getting going.

First I greet the sisters. They are in the kitchen cleaning up breakfast. There is always a small moment of anxiety, in case they tell me of some problem occurring during the night. "Is everything OK?" I ask. Everything is OK. "Poor Francis. He's been freezing.

I told him I'd take him to the thrift shop at lunch time to buy a warmer sweater," says Sister Catherine. "These California boys!" laughs Sister Peggy.

In the dining room most of the students are lingering at the dining table. I greet them warmly. "Did you sleep?" I ask. There are various nods.

"It's so quiet," says Rain, the New York City girl. "I need some noise."

The students seem relaxed. "Ohaiyo!" I say to Yorimi in Japanese. She answers at once: "Ohaiyo gozaimasu." I notice that Francis and Barbara are absent.

Barbara I find in the workspace. She has positioned the chairs in a circle.

"We don't want chairs today," I say, deciding what my warm-up will be. The first day had started with talking. The second will start with action. The others start to drift in.

At the last minute Francis appears, munching on a muffin. "Sorry," he says. "Overslept."

We stand in a circle. "Good morning, everyone. Welcome to day two. We will do lots of conducting exercises today," I say. "But first we will move our bodies. "I need it!" says Francis. "Do you know the name of the person on each side? Across?" John asks Yorimi to repeat her name.

"I have a question," says Rain. "Does the musician play during the whole scene?" "It's a good question," I answer. "Let's answer it later."

We start with Walks. Then we move on to practicing fluid sculptures, especially the conducting part.

We take a break. "Eleven minutes!" I say. Laughter. I see Yorimi looking at her watch again. When we start again (sixteen minutes later), I initiate a segment of reviewing the stories from the day before. I could choose to ask the actors how they felt on stage. There would be value in that. But again I do not want too much talking. So I take a different approach. "Let's just take that moment in the second story when the mother threw the paperweight," I say. I ask the actors from yesterday to take the stage. We all imagine that piece of floating fabric. Francis speaks: "I didn't know what to do there," he says. I invite them to try different solutions. They decide to try miming the action. I coach not only the mother, but also the teller's actor to really imagine that heavy object hitting the floor and react accordingly. They do it. It works, and the observers applaud.

"Good. I want to show something about the music. Let's go to the last moment of Sally's story. The aide has just left." I address Barbara: "What are your feelings at this moment in the scene?" I ask. "It's complicated," she replies. "I'm angry of course. And scared for her. And feeling overwhelmed. It's such a jumble." "Yes," I say.

Then I turn to Rain, sitting in the musician's spot. "Rain, can you try to play something that fits such a moment?"

"I think of something sad," she says. She looks at the range of percussion and other instruments sitting before her. Then she looks at the guitar leaning against the wall. She picks it up and plays a lovely, elegiac melody. We all look intently; we had not known she could play the guitar.

"Excellent!" I say. "Now to answer your question from before. It's usually best if the musician does not play all the time. Let's start with the exit of the aide and imagine that you have as musician been waiting for your moment, which is now. Once the aide is gone, in the silence between mother and daughter, you start to play your sad, sweet music. Barbara, you can let your body do what it wants. Maybe you will show some of your jumble of feelings. Then you say your last line."

They try it. Angel leaves with a cheery "See ya, Sweetie!" There is a moment of silence. Then the guitar starts its sad chords. Barbara looks at her mother angrily. Then moves to another part of the room to straighten up. Then looks at her mother again, this time with a more resigned expression. Rain stops playing. Barbara sighs. "Goodbye, Mother," she says. "It's been lovely." "Yes, dear," says Francis as the mother.

"Great!" I say. We could all feel it. "Good going, everyone." It is time for lunch. I reflect to myself that Barbara, so contained, so quiet, has now been chosen twice as the teller's actor. And she has fulfilled the roles with surprising effectiveness. But before we end,

I turn to Sally, sitting in the audience. "We've just gone back to your story of yesterday. Why don't you have the last word?" Sally looks grateful for the chance to speak. "I felt uncertain afterward because I love my mother, and I worried that my story was not fair to her. The music is good. I did have so many feelings at that time, but I could feel my love in the music."

At lunch we sit looking out at the frozen Hudson River, talking of this and that. Naturally playback is also a topic. Angel asks about playback and youth. Sally mentions her playback performances in the library and asks if I have experience with playback in that setting. I give short disquisitions in reply. Sometimes I am glad for such questions, for it can be a good moment for informal teaching. But at other times, I'd rather relax and chat.

Taking my dirty dishes into the kitchen, I find myself next to Barbara. "Good acting," I tell her. She says nothing, but it is clear she is pleased by the recognition.

In the afternoon we continue with exercises about conducting the short forms. We do a fluid sculpture segment and a pairs segment. During the pairs exercise, there is a moment of danger. John, paired with Angel, elbows her in the torso. She yells out in pain, and everything stops. She looks at him sharply. He apologizes. I make remarks about actors needing to be in control of their energy. When we are set to continue, Angel says she would like to change partners. There is a sense of discord in the room. I am watching John carefully, who is now the isolated one. But he seems to be carrying on without a problem.

As we are sorting out who will take the stage for a playback story, Angel asks to be the teller. Francis, a little to my surprise, offers to conduct, with Barbara, Rain, and Sally as actors and Yorimi on music. John is in the audience.

What Angel tells about is an encounter with police during her stay in the United States, who stop her without warning when she is returning from a concert. Francis does not ask many questions, but he does ascertain that there are two policemen, both white, both men. "They go over my passport and ask for my visa papers. Do you think I carry my visa papers with me every day? They search everything in my handbag," she says. "Even my tampons.

They ask if I am carrying drugs. Then they make me lean against their car and pat me down. They turn me around and tell me to snap my bra to make sure nothing is hidden inside it. I was so angry and upset. But I said nothing. I could barely speak. I was worried they would take me in to check on my immigration status. But they let me go."

Francis turns the story over to the actors. The musician plays. The scene unfolds. Rain plays Angel. She is cheery, then silent, then sullen. Barbara and Sally play the police. They follow the story, but lack menace. They do not embody male threatening energy.

When it is finished, Francis asks Angel for confirmation. She says it felt worse than that. He makes a comment that even what they showed looked pretty awful. Angel laughs, and says, "I'd just like to kick their fat asses!" Francis hesitates, then thanks her for her story.

As discussion starts, Angel turns to John, who is sitting next to her. "I don't hold anything against you," she says. "That story just came up."

"I'm no fan of the cops," he replies. "But I know my energy is intimidating sometimes." He pauses. "It's a theme of my life." It is the most vulnerable thing he has said during the workshop. There are surely many stories there. But there is no time for another story today.

We then talk about the place of playback theatre as a kind of people's history and the importance of voicing truth. There is also discussion of the ending of Angel's story.

"Couldn't we have done what she said and added a scene where she kicks their asses?" Rain asks. "It's so depressing to leave it this way!"

"It is certainly possible," I tell her. "We used to do it frequently in the early days. But sometimes the unredeemed truth is what needs to be dramatized. We can ask Angel." I turn to her. "What do you think? Would you have liked to see that extra scene where you get back at them?"

Angel laughs. "I like the idea," she says. "But I think it was good the way it was. We need to know how it is," she adds.

When Sally comments that she had trouble really getting into the role of the policeman, I agree with her. I ask them to stand up and suggest we practice. And for the last exercise of the day, we practice embodying large men who are not kind. There is laughter, but also moments of tense application (after all, everyone has their own experience of dealing with violent or malicious men). When it is over, they relax as if they have just had a workout.

I say to the students, "If we cannot embody the darkness in someone's story, they will not feel heard."

"It can't always be a love cocoon," says Barbara.

"Literature is full of evil," says John.

"Or life?" says Angel.

It is time to end the day. We circle up. I say, "Good going!" I take my leave.

That night, in bed, I hear their voices in my mind as I ease toward sleep: Yorimi's accented English, Angel's strong voice and musical expressions, each way of talking. It is as if they are insisting on talking to me. Or am I insisting on keeping up a conversation with them?

Encounter with Nothing

We are halfway through the Conducting workshop. I arrive for day three almost half an hour early, mainly out of eagerness. I bring with me a copy of a book about the American dance pioneer Doris Humphreys for Francis, who receives it with one of his sweet smiles.

This day we start with talking. I ask the students for any reflections or personal statements about how they are doing in the workshop. Everyone has something to say, including Angel, who says that even though she gets very angry at the racism she sees and sometimes experiences, she is very glad to be able to be studying in the United States.

Then I invite a physical warm-up. Angel offers. She puts on some lively calypso music and leads the group in fifteen minutes of the most vigorous and challenging hip-shaking dance. Her voice is transformed. We can hardly understand what she says, but her movements make it clear what she wants. In no time at all we are joyfully dancing this dance we cannot properly do.

The main task of the morning is to do stories in two small sub-groups. It is a chance, I say, for everyone to be conductor. I suggest we divide up by age, the young ones together (Francis, Yorimi, Angel), and the older ones together (Barbara, Sally, Rain, John). I give some guidelines about enacting stories with one or two actors.

This is one of my perennial exercises. I know that in the intimacy of the small group, perhaps without the teacher watching, people often do their best work. They also often tell tender stories.

While the groups, in separate rooms, do the exercise, I sit in the hallway, half-listening. I always remain on hand, in case I am needed for any reason. But usually I am not. I become an invisible witness to moments of laughter, tears, applause. I know that I have been a catalyst for this energy, but it is deeply satisfying that they are undertaking such a highly engaged exchange entirely without me.

After lunch I suggest we do more playback stories in the whole group. I invite Sally, as the most experienced, to be conductor. I suggest that anyone who did not act in yesterday's whole group stories be an actor. John steps up. Yorimi says: "I should go to the stage, but I have a story." I tell her it is fine. Rain goes.

Angel and Francis look at each other.

"You go," Francis says. He laughs: "I need my rest."

Angel takes the stage. Barbara goes to the musician's place.

All are ready. There is a pause. Finally Yorimi says: "I am in a conflict with my mother."

"A conflict?" asks Sally.

"She thinks I should be doing more with my life."

"Doing more?"

"Finishing university, getting work."

"What kind of work?"

Here I interrupt, for I see the pattern. Sally is practicing reflective listening rather than active conducting. "Let's start again. This time I want you to make the first move."

Such an intervention on my part risks alienating Sally, who has her pride as leader of a PT company, but I think she can take it. She is smiling weakly. "Again," I say.

This time Sally is first to speak. "Where does your story take place?"

"Good!" I interject.

"In Japan," says Yorimi.

"Where in Japan?"

"Good!" I interject again. "The actors need a setting, a specific setting.

"In my home," answers Yorimi.

"What happens?" asks Sally. She is in a better groove now.

"My mother and I are eating our evening meal. She is not saying anything, but I know she is angry. I am not saying anything, either. I'm not hungry."

"And then?"

"That's it."

"Nothing else happens?"

"Nothing else."

"What do you do instead of university or a job?"

"Good!" I say. "You are being a story detective."

"I sit in my room."

"Just sit in your room."

"Yes."

"Doing anything?"

"Sometimes I just lie on my bed. Sometimes I play video games."

"This is your story, then," says Sally, as she turns to the actors. Suddenly she realizes she has forgot to cast the characters. "Oh! Please pick someone to be you and your mother." Yorimi picks Angel for her, and Rain for the mother.

"What is a word for you in the story?" Sally asks.

"Nothing."

Sally seems not sure what this answer means. She hesitates. Then simply repeats, "Nothing. Let's watch."

The setting-up music begins as the actors take their places. Yorimi is in her room, lying on a bed. The mother is on the other side of the stage. Mother calls to daughter: "Yorimi, time to go to class!" Yorimi does not move. Mother moves about the house and then calls again. "Yorimi, you have an exam today!" Yorimi, still on the bed, does not move. Then she gets up and goes to a computer. John, who has been waiting, comes suddenly to life, making loud sounds of pistol shots and various sound effects. The audience laughs. Mother calls: "Yorimi! You have that interview." Yorimi keeps playing. She lies down on the bed again. Much time seems to pass. "Yorimi, dinner!" Yorimi sighs, gets up, leaves her room. She sits at the dinner table. Mother, glowering, puts the food on. She starts to eat, then notices that Yorimi has scarcely taken a mouthful. "Yorimi," she admonishes. "Eat!" Yorimi sits with slumped shoulders. The musician sounds a Tibetan bell to mark the end of the scene, and the actors look up and over to the teller.

We look at Sally and Yorimi.

"Did you see your story?"

"Yes, I did," says Yorimi. "It is just like that."

A story similar to that of many Japanese young people, I happen to know. The actors have done quite a good job. "Good going, everyone," I say. "Let's talk about this a little bit." By now I am taking a different approach than at the start, encouraging reflection. I ask Sally how it felt. She apologizes for the first attempt, but says the second go felt more on track. I agree, and I praise her for not needing to ask more questions, but instead getting it over to the actors. I comment that Yorimi's "nothing," while not totally clear, was very evocative of her state. I praise Rain for her choices as the mother, particularly the time compression.

"I wasn't chosen for anything," says John. "So I took a role."

"That's fine, that's what we do," I answer.

"I chose the video game."

"An excellent choice," I say to John. "The challenge is not to overdo it and make the scene comic. You reined it in just at the right time." To Angel: "Of course you chose when to go to the computer and when to stop. You had a good feel for it," I say.

Diagnosis

Yorimi, although she has said so little, has revealed a lot. There is a thickness in the atmosphere.

At this moment of alert engagement, I take about five minutes to speak about the connections between the stories. Within the playback theatre world, we call it the red thread, I say. I point out the associations: the first story (John's) is about reluctant students, and so is the fourth (Yorimi's). The second story is told by a daughter about her mother, and so is the fourth. In stories two, three, and four anger has been a strong presence. Our stories are connected in so many ways, I say; we are weaving a web together, a web of stories.

Rain says she would like to conduct. I nod. Sally and Yorimi join John on stage.

Francis comes slowly. "I guess it has to be me," he says with a little laugh.

"It doesn't have to be you," I say quickly. "I don't want you to feel forced to be the teller." But his emotion is visible.

"It's OK," he says, sitting on the teller's chair. Rain looks at him and gives him a big grin. Perhaps she hasn't noticed his seriousness? "What is a color for your story?" she asks. This is a formulation that she has learned somewhere.

"Red and gray," Francis answers.

"Where does it take place?" asks Rain, still smiling.

"I don't know," he says.

"It has to take place somewhere!" she says.

"OK. In a dance audition. In freshman year."

"Fantastic!" she says. "Pick an actor to be you."

Francis looks at the row of actors, John, Yorimi, Sally, and hesitates. "Yorimi," he says. She stands, as she is supposed to, in a position of attentiveness.

"What happens?" asks the conductor.

Francis begins his narrative: "It was the winter of freshman year and there was this audition for a dance performance that I really wanted to be in. I had just got my diagnosis, and I was supposed to avoid too much activity. But I didn't care. I really wanted to be in this piece."

"Oh, dance, I love dance!" says Rain, again, her voice full of gaiety, as if she has not heard that word "diagnosis."

"What happens?" she asks.

"We are asked to do a move in groups of three. It is very physical. I fall down, because I'm weak." He gives his little laugh. "Obviously I didn't get accepted."

"That's it?"

"Yes," he sighs.

"OK," says Rain.

"We'll see your story now. The other actors can fill in as necessary. Let's watch."

She leans back in her chair, as Barbara the musician starts the setting-up music.

I feel compelled to intervene. I ask Rain: "Did you hear what he said?"

"What do you mean?" She looks at me, puzzled.

I hesitate to say the word baldly, but Francis says it for me: "Diagnosis."

"Oh, diagnosis," says Rain. She pauses. "I didn't really take it in," she says.

"Take it in now," I urge her. My brief acquaintance with Francis plays before my eyes: the almost bald head; the scarf, Sister Catherine taking him to buy warmer clothing, his sleeping late.

"What are you thinking?" I ask her.

"I don't want to take it in. I don't want it to be true. Maybe it is cancer, or something. Like leukemia."

"It's worse than that," says Francis. "Multiple myeloma."

"Oh," says Rain, in a very changed voice. I look around the room. Everyone is looking intently at Francis. I am stunned. I know that multiple myeloma is virtually incurable. I also know my job is be the guide. I say to Rain: "You don't want it to be true. But it is true. Perhaps that is the heart of the story, not only for you, but for the teller in his narrative. What else do you need to know? What more do you want to ask?"

Rain looks like she is about to cry. "I don't know," she says. "I don't want to ask him anything more."

"He came to the chair because he wants to tell his story," I tell her. I cast a look at Francis. He nods.

"I'm not so good with serious stories," she says.

"Ask him about his illness. Ask for details."

She looks at Francis. She takes his hand. We can see how hard it is for her. "Tell me about it," she says, almost in a whisper.

Francis replies in a normal voice. "I had been with surprisingly low energy and my left leg started to swell up. They took some tests, and told me I had this serious form of cancer."

Rain looks at me. "Do you need to know more?" I ask her.

"When he found out?" she asks me.

"Good," I tell her. "Continue."

She takes a deep breath, then asks Francis: "When did you learn you had multiple myeloma?"

"It was just a little before this. I hadn't even got the full treatment plan yet. I was kind of in denial, I guess."

"So this is part of the story," says Rain, now on track.

"Yes," he answers. "It is."

"Let's watch," says Rain abruptly, turning it over to the actors. They are surprised, expecting more words, more information. "Is your mother important?" asks John from the stage.

I intervene at once, since one of the rules of the playback ritual is that actors never ask questions. "You don't need to know anything more. Just do your best," I say. I give them a hint: "You can play more than one role, if you want."

The music starts. We see Yorimi alone on the stage. She is dancing to herself. But then she tires and sits down. It is hard not to hear an echo of her own recent story, so full of fatigue. John comes onto the stage. He is holding a piece of cloth like a clipboard, and looking at it. "Mr. Smith," he says. "I have some results for you. They are positive, I'm afraid." The teller's actor comes over to that part of the stage now the doctor's office. "What?" "You have a form of cancer very unusual in one so young. Chemotherapy. Bone marrow transplant. Live a careful life." The teller's actor listens, stunned. "Goodbye," says the doctor abruptly. Francis is alone again on stage. He wanders slowly, shaking his head. We see Sally enter upstage right. She is also holding a piece of cloth as a clipboard (a nice touch, I think to myself). "This is a modern dance piece that will have its premier at this college," she says, very briskly. "We will have a six-week rehearsal period. Line up over here." She gestures to her left. John has re-entered, obviously as a dancer. Yorimi joins him. "Just walk across, please. I want to see how you move." The two actors cross the stage. John cannot resist a moment of humor, as he exaggerates a dancer's fluid walk.

Yorimi walks without affectation and looks graceful because of it. The director marks her clipboard. "Now in pairs," she says. "I want you to do something big and strong together." The dancers start to move across the stage, now as a pair. John leans on Yorimi, who struggles to hold him, then falls to the ground. The director writes. "Next!" she says. As the music plays — this time a gentle xylophone — Yorimi sits alone on the stage. She cries out: "I want to dance!" The scene is over. Yorimi looks up and over at Francis.

After a pause Rain asks Francis: "Did you see your story?"

"Even things I didn't say. The doctor who told me that I had cancer was so cold about it, just like this doctor," he says.

"Is there anything else you want to add?" Rain asks.

"Good," I interrupt. She is not dismissing him too abruptly. The teller needs time; we all need time.

"That was a year ago," he said. "I've gone through two rounds of chemotherapy, and I'm going to have a bone marrow transplant this summer."

Rain gives Francis a hug. "Thank you for your story," she says. Francis goes back to the audience.

There is a heavy silence in the room. "Let's take a short pause," I say. "I'm going to play some music. Take time just to make contact with Francis, or anyone else." I put on Erik Satie. People are giving Francis and each other hugs. There are some whispered words. After a few minutes, I stop the music and bring people back together. "Good going, everyone," I say. "Thank you, Francis, for your story. Now we'll take a proper break."

"How many minutes?" asks John playfully.

"We'll know when it's time to come back," I answer in the same spirit.

As I sip my coffee, standing a little apart, I have many feelings. Full of tenderness for Francis, this lithe but shadowed youth. For Yorimi, as well, who told her story of depression, then rose to a big challenge as an actor. I am content; even though the conducting and the acting were far from perfect, we could all feel the power of the stories. I start to organize thoughts for discussion as I watch carefully, gauging the atmosphere, seeing how people are. They are drinking, nibbling, talking, hugging. It seems OK.

When we come back from the break, I have put on Zakir Hussain's *Toni*, with its seductive, slow melody. I tell them we will do some talking in a minute, but first let the music move through them as they dance. As we all move together, there is lots of eye contact, and people move fluidly from solo to duet formation. At one point there is even a group of three moving together. I notice that Francis is fully engaged, moving his body with abandon. The piece comes to an end, and stillness fills the room.

"Let's sit in a circle," I say. I want people to be able to see each other.

Sally speaks first. "I was unsure when to come in as the dance director," she says. "I couldn't find the right timing."

"It was fine," I reply. "You might have waited a bit longer to allow the teller's actor to react more to the news from the doctor," I say. "But it was basically OK." I want to give useful feedback to Sally. At the same time, I know that this discussion can leap off in a second into an ill-advised breast-beating and fault-finding session.

Yorimi speaks: "I am sorry," she says. "I could not play Francis."

"Don't say that!" says Francis. "You played me very well." Others concur.

"I am not a dancer."

"Perhaps not," I say. "But you inhabited his role. We could see him through you."

"I was so blocked as the conductor," says Rain. "I just freaked out." I look at her, with her oversized earrings and bright clothes. "That's why you're here, Rain," I say. "To learn to never freak out. To keep it moving forward. To stay at the helm at all times. A serious story can come at any time. You have to be ready."

"It's terrifying," she says.

"The audience can quickly become anxious if the moment is not held properly. That's also why the actors never ask questions." I look at John, who starts to challenge me,

"But..."

"There is no 'But,'" I say. "We cannot afford to lose the forward momentum. You need to trust that you have enough information. The musician is also so important in this kind of scene." I nod at Barbara. Once more I turn to Rain. "You are a person who likes brightness and good cheer," I say. "But some stories are painted in somber colors. If you can't accept the dark as well as the bright, then I want you to think about whether playback theatre is for you." She looks at me with a kind of stricken look. "But you are here," I repeat. "I applaud you for that."

"And I want to compliment you, John," I say. "You have a good feel for stories. You embodied the TV in Yorimi's story. In Francis's you played the roles necessary to make the story work."

"Thank you," he says.

Rain raises her hand. "Don't we need something more?" she asks. "Both stories were so ...unhappy. Don't the tellers need to see something positive?" It is the "happy ending" question again, this time implicitly connected to a common fear of leaving the teller too open.

I turn to the tellers. "Let's ask them how they feel, " I say.

"I am glad to tell," says Yorimi. "I feel more light, not so heavy, even though my story is heavy."

"Me, too," says Francis. "I feel I can be myself with you now."

As we wrap up, I urge John to watch out for hamming, noting his stereotyped dancer's walk, and I compliment Sally on her taking up John's idea of the cloth clipboard.

I am also aware we now have an unfolding here-and-now story in the group: living with an ill member. "Francis, did you write about your illness on the new student form?"

He shakes his head. "I was afraid you would tell me not to come."

"It's never good to be reckless," I answer. "Tell us. In the remaining time of this workshop, what can you do and not do? How can we support you?"

"Just don't lean on me too hard!" he laughs. "No, seriously, I get tired sometimes. And I need to take care of myself. That's all."

John, with his ever-masculine energy, tosses him a throw rug that has been on the sofa. "Here!" he says.

Francis ignores it. "I'm fine," he says. Then he adds in a softer voice: "I'm here because I refuse to give up. I had to take the semester off because of the treatments. But I felt could come to this. I thought I could handle this."

We are almost finished, and it will be good for the students to have a little down time before dinner.

"Just let yourself notice the red thread," I say. "A story on the first day took place at college (John's), as did Francis's; that is association. Today, however, the first story takes place at "not college" (Yorimi's, who refused to go). We call that opposition. There is also another very big opposition: Sally told a story about her mother, an old person who was ill. Today there was a kind of response from Francis. Not all people dealing with physical problems are old, he is reminding us. This is how we carry on a dialogue through our stories."

I suddenly gesture at the group with my hands. "OK. Everybody up!" I rush over and put on a lively African song, Coco M'bassi's *Muengue Mwa Ndolo*. "Walk!" I instruct. "Not alone! With at least one other!" I say. They are happy to get up, happy for the change of mood, happy for the beat. "Switch. Find a new person to walk with." They can't resist talking as they are walking. "Switch once more, for the last time!" I say. After about fifteen seconds, I gently fade the music.

I gesture for us to stand in a circle. "That's it for today," I tell them. "Good work. I'll be going home. Remember, tomorrow is the last day, and it is short. We end at lunch. See you in the morning."

They clap desultorily. I leave the room, while they are still standing there. I could easily linger. But I know I also need my peace. I drive home past the supermarket, the gas stations. I hardly register the cars on the highway. My mind is full of images from Falling Waters and the intense stories we have shared. An eighteen-wheeler pulls by me. I had better think about the road, I tell myself.

On the fourth day I arrive forty minutes early. I sit and have breakfast with the students. The sun shines over the frozen river. The students tell me they sang songs late into the night. After tears comes the lightness and the laughter, I think to myself, with a twinge of regret that I was not there, too.

Two people in the group, John and Yorimi, have not conducted. "My research project!" says John, to justify his getting a chance. Although we cannot always satisfy everyone, even in this theatre of inclusion, I invite them both to conduct, but not full stories. We do a narrative short form called three-part story, and they both get their chance. I give John direct feedback, because I know he will expect it. With Yorimi, so self-critical herself, I am gentle. To the actors, I give some very light comments. For we are at the end. There will be no more time to follow up.

At the break I urge Angel privately to keep going with playback theatre. I tell her she has a lot of promise.

We start a closure process that will last longer than an hour. It involves action. It involves talking. It involves review of our formal learning. It involves reflecting, both personally and cognitively. We come to a final round of the circle, a time for each person, as at the start, to be seen and heard. I ask them for the standout aspect of their experience.

Barbara: "I didn't know if I could do it, be a cop violating a woman. I almost asked to sit down. Then I thought of the sisters. I know. It doesn't seem connected. But they never rest. They say they are having a group of forty coming next week. They never ask to sit down. They get on with it. They just do it. 'Just do it.' That's what I'm taking with me."

Angel: "I like this possibility for dialogue."

Rain: "I feel more courageous. I want to be more courageous."

Yorimi: "Thank you to everyone for your patience. I could not speak. And I want to thank our teacher for the way he listens."

John: "Like Yorimi, I will take home a resolve to listen more. To look and listen. And to watch my energy when I am doing pairs!"

Sally: "I am thinking about John's research project, which focuses on dramatizing moments from literature and combining it with playback. I think I could do that at my library."

Francis: "I am light. I am lucky. I am alive."

I always take part in this final circle of comments. My urge is to talk about Matthew, my little brother. But he died, and I do not want to impose my experience on young Francis. Suppressing that, I am momentarily stuck. "I love doing playback in sight of such a huge and majestic river," I say.

All of a sudden it is over. When I get home, I store the cloth, the instruments, and the cubes in our garage. The whole effort has been like putting together a jigsaw puzzle. I bring some of the pieces; the students each bring some pieces. Then we try to put them together in a way that will make coherent whole, a pleasing design.

What was the main focus? Was it the curriculum, the role training, the stories, the connecting? The starting from zero? Conducting as safe rite of passage? And I always seem to be trying to find the equilibrium between talking and not-talking (that is, movement, music, and silence).

Those negative feelings at the start of worry (low numbers) and frustration (no really experienced conductors or even actors) are distant now. I am already missing these people, who were unknown to me before. So many of their stories were painful, but they were the opposite of depressing. To the contrary. I am strangely uplifted by Yorimi's story of her lethargy and isolation, by Angel's of everyday police brutality, by Sally's of struggling with her aging mother, and by Francis's story of illness and resolve that reminds me of my own.

Lying down on the warm bed in the late afternoon sunlight, I realize suddenly that none of us ever called him "Spider." I shut my eyes and let the river of sleep wash my teacher's thoughts away.

Chapter Eleven

School II

I really didn't want to move. I liked our barn in the woods. But the number of students was growing too fast. We couldn't find enough neighbors with spare rooms to put them up. Jo urged finding a larger residential facility for our trainings.

The choice was Vassar College, twenty-one miles away. It meant a daily commute for us, but the students would all reside on site, and we would run our school on the campus of a prestigious American university.

In the fourteen years we stayed at Vassar the students consistently approved. They liked the gardens and the elegance (we held our graduations in the "Rose Parlor," a burgundy-carpeted room with period furniture, where we handed each graduating student a rose along with their diploma). But for us it was not so easy.

Many is the time, for instance, that we showed up to our classroom, ready and eager to jump into theatre practice, to find it locked. The students then milled about as we called the security office (our relationship with Vassar coincided with the arrival of mobile phones—we couldn't have functioned there without them). We might have to wait ten or fifteen minutes to have the door opened, only to walk in and find that the room had been used the night before by another group and left uncleaned. We straightened up as best we could, but in the process lost precious time and energy.

We were one of many summer programs—that is, not formally affiliated with Vassar—often competing with each other for workspaces. There was a large bureaucracy, itself with competing departments; the buildings and grounds department, for example, often ignored the needs of the summer program department, and even worse than finding our classroom uncleaned, we might learn it was suddenly unavailable due to a renovation project. No sooner had we begun the first Leadership class than jackhammers started up outside the window, and we ended up having to use a foyer in the science building as our workspace for the entire three weeks.

At Vassar the playback students stayed in student apartments. When the regular college students left for their summer vacation, these spaces were stripped bare, which meant that we ourselves needed to equip them with bed linens and kitchenware, toilet brushes and brooms — all the necessities. Buying the stuff was the easy part. Installing it at the start of each summer, then lugging it all away at the end — these tasks almost gave us permanent back trouble. The apartments were invariably left dirty, which meant a rigorous cleaning job as well. We were such a small organization. It meant, in fact, that a large part of what needed to be done was handled by myself, Jo, and our office assistant.

In time we learned how to deal. We established our own protocols to handle the college bureaucracy. But I missed the small and simple barn, encircled by hayfields, with students camping under tents.

Larger classes (our first year at Vassar in 1994 we had a combined group of twenty-seven for the two- and three-week advanced courses) also tested our knowledge of how to manage groups. For instance, I gave the students the challenge of staging playback theatre performances for the campus public, with the two classes working together in mixed groups. Then unaccountably I decided not to attend them, saying to myself that the students should be able to manage on their own. When one of these shows did not go well, recriminations and bad feelings ensued. Back in their separate sections, with those being criticized not necessarily present, the students' mood plummeted. A sticky situation became almost unmanageable. Most serious of all, I could not use the performances as a teachable moment because I had not been there.

From this failure we learned some valuable lessons. From that time on the staff considered all performances a major part of their responsibility. The whole community — students and staff — held short community meetings every morning whether there were problems or not, in order to keep open communication. And we limited the size of our classes to fifteen.

The School offerings were progressive. After Core Training, each class had its prerequisite. Of course for the initial Leadership class, there was no question of making one's way through the School because the School was new. I invited a wide group of mostly company leaders to join the first graduating class. The first cohort of nine came from five countries; the non-Americans were all founders of playback in their countries.

One participant was a professor who the day before the graduation said, "I've received many certificates and diplomas in my life; I couldn't care less about another graduation." But we have a photo of him holding his diploma and his rose after our graduation ceremony with a distinctly happy look on his face.

The youngest was a recent college graduate who had first seen playback theatre as a thirteen-year-old at a summer event in her own country. Not only had she never forgotten, but playback theatre was to become a focus for her life.

Restoring the Balance

I kept asking Jo to teach courses, and it was not long before the School's "sole proprietor" basis just did not feel right. So in 1995 I formally asked her to co-direct the whole operation with me. After all, we were used to working together through the years of the original company. The questionable side of this shift was reliance on an old pattern: depending on her often behind-the-scenes support. The positive side was a recognition that at bottom I was more interested in collaboration than autocracy. Jo agreed to the new status. So the Jonathan Fox School of Playback Theatre became simply the School of Playback Theatre, and my life realigned a notch with my philosophy.

As in the original company, Jo's skills complemented mine. Her standards were rigorous, her execution thorough. She had already shown herself to be a gifted teacher, very different in style, but allied totally in our mission to train skilled and ethical playback theatre performers. We collaborated at every level, from discussing where to place students, to producing fliers, to orchestrating the graduation.

Freewheeling in my approach, I chafed at the idea of too much planning and evaluation. But under Jo's influence, each year after the summer program was over we engaged in a full two-day review. These sessions were exhausting (especially since we were still depleted from our summer labors), but the location helped: sitting on a grassy hillside on the small island in Maine where we took our holiday, gazing at sea, islands, and the occasional seal.

Together we built a training program that at its height served more than one hundred students annually. In 2002 we added a ten-day winter program. Each autumn with the help of our one staff member and Jo, I put together the program for the coming year. Classes were well enough attended to enable us to fly in some of our most admired colleagues from Down Under: Francis Batten, Christian Penny, Peter Hall, and most often, Bev Hosking. We invited psychodramatist Judy Swallow, our compatriot in the original company; Sarah Halley, an organizational consultant and expert in race awareness, along with her colleague, Pamela Freeman, an African-American social worker; a British actress from Hong Kong, Veronica Needa, who would become a staunch ambassador for playback, especially in Asia, and a close collaborator; and our daughter Hannah, who showed a natural talent for teaching.

Attending the School was a big contrast to an evening rehearsal or a two-day workshop. You could come and stay for a week or two and take progressively more challenging courses. We worked hard to embody in our teaching the very principles of respect and collaboration that underpinned the playback idea. Since the students used their personal stories as the material for study and they came from all over—from about fifteen different countries in a typical year—we had an exceptionally rich field for learning, both about playback and about the world.

As the word spread, we began to attract students from Eastern Europe and Africa. The 1990s predated a world that was electronically connected, and the wide geographical pull of the School often meant long and complicated communications by mail and phone, often with official bodies.

We had challenges, of course, often caused by cultural and economic difference. One year a group of Finns moved into a student apartment that had been occupied during the previous course by Brazilians. They found the place a complete mess. Even though we made it clear to students that it was their responsibility to leave their living space clean for the next group, these middle-class Brazilians, used to having servants look after them, could not adjust.

More serious was the communal dinner that the students decided to organize on the last night of a certain class. In the middle of enjoying a huge pot of spaghetti, they noticed one member was absent. Upon searching, they found him locked in his room because he was too poor to chip in his share of the expenses. They begged him to join them, saying the money did not matter. But he did not come out that night.

The biggest issue, of course, was tuition cost, beyond the reach of all but the moneyed class in many countries. From the start we had offered scholarships, deciding after hearing a person's story what we could do for them. However, the School had become too big for such an ad hoc approach. Furthermore, our insistence on small classes meant that the margin between breaking even and enough profit for modest growth was very narrow, and we had to monitor carefully how much we could give away. Knowing that every scholarship meant less income for me and Jo did not stop us. We treasured this rich convocation of nations, and of course, spreading playback theatre throughout the world, including to poorer countries, was part of our founders' mission.

The Face Onstage

Our method of allocating scholarships was not foolproof. I remember a lady who asked for a reduction, then arrived in a new Mercedes; another who headed directly after our training for a meditation retreat, which was expensive and offered no scholarships (the operating philosophy there was if you want it badly enough, you will be able to manifest the money"). Naiveté led us to give them support, and we were later to tighten up our allocations process. But we were also operating from a polar-opposite conviction. By virtue of the accident of birth and the inequity of our societies, not everyone could "manifest" the funds to take playback theatre training. If playback theatre were ever to outgrow its white, middle-class roots, a certain level of social awareness was essential.

There was another reason why such awareness was important. Without it, the prejudices of mainstream society would be replicated on the playback stage, and Jo and I did not want that. An example:

A woman tells about her jumble of emotions going on a first date — being unable to eat from nervousness and also very excited. The conductor (a male trainee) makes an assumption that the date is with a man, and the teller corrects him, stating her date was another woman. After the enactment, she comments that she saw a look of disgust on some actors' faces that was not congruent with her feeling (which was not nausea but simply absence of hunger). The conductor, sensing her unhappiness, asked her for a clarification. The teller emphasized the excitement and joy of the moment. What emerged in discussion afterward was the teller's sense of being manipulated into coming out and her concern that the "disgust" she saw portrayed did not have to do with her story but with the actors' reaction to her identity. It was possibly true.

To be confronted with actors' prejudice derailed the teller's purpose in recounting her story — to share with others a vivid and wonderful personal moment.

A playback theatre performer without social awareness may offend tellers — or audience members — with an interpretation that is myopic or worse. Most of the time, especially if the teller either is not offered a chance to express her dissatisfaction or is too polite to, the actors will never know. (Without the first-date teller's courage to speak up, her concerns would never have emerged.)

The "shooting gallery" blunder was one occasion on which I was made aware of my own ignorance. But how many times, both as conductor and actor, was I oblivious? How many times because of my own lack of awareness did I alienate, or worse, offend a teller or members of the audience?

At a certain point it became important for me to increase my awareness. In the early 1990s, Jo was part of a study group of whites and blacks taking place in our small town. Its purpose was to read articles and talk about racism. I joined them. The discussions were rambling and often without much insight. But the experience, biweekly talks over three years, changed my outlook. Perhaps just openly facing certain questions rather than avoiding them was enough. After taking part in the study group, when I conducted African-Americans in playback theatre, a reticence, I might say even fear, was gone. Before I had held back, conscious of myself as a white who avoided issues of race. Now I was more aware of potential points of difference and I could use my story sense to ask questions that touched directly on the wounds of historical past or the pain of an unjust present.

I remembered the African-American teller, who said: "It's not *my* Fourth of July." It never really felt like mine, either. (At university I had read about the speech of the renowned nineteenth century black abolitionist Frederick Douglass, "The Meaning of July Fourth for the Negro," but had conveniently forgotten it; not until someone raised the topic face-to-face in playback theatre years later did its truth stick with me, not only for the African-American teller, but for myself.[14]

At the international playback theatre conference that took place in Olympia, Washington, in 1995 I did a storytelling performance. On stage with me were Jo as musician, Hannah as a dancer, and serving as a traditional storyteller, an African-American multi-talented professor of education and strong proponent of black rights, JohnL Johnson.

I had gone through my usual warm-up process and had decided on a children's song as an opener. Even adults usually liked to join in the chorus, and the silliness of it might help me get into a groove. But standing backstage just before the start, I looked at JohnL, thought of my song, and decided I had better check with him.

"I'm planning to open with a silly song." I said. "It's called Matilda the Gorilla. What do you think?"

As he paused to answer, I could picture the song, its ape-like movements, JohnL on stage being pressured to join in, the popular defamation comparing blacks with monkeys, and I cringed that I

126

had even considered singing Matilda this particular night.

JohnL slowly shook his head. "Do you have another possibility?" he asked gently.

"Of course," I said, both relieved and panicked at the same time. My opening gone! Now what? A minute later, we started.

JohnL signed up for the "Playback Theatre and Social Change" workshop I offered later that year. I debated with myself beforehand whether I had the right (or adequate knowledge) to propose such a theme. But I went ahead anyway.

I remember there were ten whites and two African-Americans in that workshop. Presented with the subject of discrimination, the white participants were eager to tell stories about prejudice in their families and also when as a child they first encountered prejudice. Meanwhile the blacks held back. It was getting toward the end of the workshop. My anxiety level rose. Was I not able to facilitate an atmosphere where *all* were willing to speak up? This was the whole point of the workshop, and there was not much time left. I did know there was no magic recipe. If I were too demanding, or too insensitive, I knew JohnL would not save me, and rightly so. The two blacks were undoubtedly skeptical of the innocent-observer stance of the white participants. In addition we were consciously working against the institutionalized forces of the society, which taught in a hundred ways that the African-American narrative was tiresome, depressing, provocative, or even dangerous.

In the end JohnL told a story about his grandfather. I will never forget it. It was a not untypical tale about blatant discrimination in the workplace and also great dignity in the face of it. What made it so shocking was the personal aspect, revealing a searing chapter in the history of the teller's family.

Still reverberating from that final tale, I breathed a sigh of relief after the workshop was over. We had done it (or rather JohnL had done it). We had not retreated into anecdotes from the above-stairs crowd. But I was also left with an unease. A social change workshop with only two people of color, and I had strained my capacity even to enlist the participation of those two (one had never seen playback theatre before and was very shy about the theatre part). Ten and two was not a salubrious ratio.

I also gradually became more aware of reasons why a teller might be reticent to tell.

An example:

I am in a playback theatre training in New Zealand, interviewing a teller, who is Maori. We do not know it yet, but the story will be a shocking testament of injustice perpetrated by (white) government officials. I say, "Pick someone to play you in the story." The teller looks up, sees four actors, three white and one Maori, looking at her from the stage and bursts into tears. It takes a while to find out why. "It is the first time I have ever had the chance to pick someone like me," she says.

Without that Maori actor, the teller might not have dared to tell her story.

We routinely do a segment of teaching in our trainings called the "face of the story," which aims to expand students' capacity to hear the archetypal and societal dimensions of everyday personal stories. The idea is that we can see it all in the "face of the story," just as the teller tells it. The Maori teller brings to our awareness the importance of another kind of face, having nothing to do with the story itself, but the face of the actor — simply having a brother or sister onstage ready to act for you, one from a world like yours.[16]

In my conducting workshop how different would the atmosphere have been had Angel not been the only person of color? If she had been able to pick a black-skinned person to play her, how would her narrative have changed? More importantly, how would the enactment have differed? And if there had been other brothers and sisters to respond, to share their experiences, how would that have changed the group dynamic?

In our work in the original company, we had gone to the prisons, which in the United States house mostly people of color. From a belief in reaching out to even the most marginalized tellers, we had exposed ourselves to personal searches and the claustrophobic experience of locked chambers. (Of course an agency paid us to do this.) But beyond that, what did we do?

We never conceived of the possibility that if we were interested in working in prisons, it would make our commitment more authentic, and our work more effective, if we included among our actors individuals who knew the life of prisoners and their families. To do that would have required so much time, so much effort. We would have had to make connections with prisoner groups. We would have had to get to know ex-offenders. We would have had to confront in our own cohort the systemic racism that lands so many people of color behind bars as well as other entrenched social forces that keep whites and people of color apart in the United States. It was enough for us just to pull off our weekly rehearsals. How could we spend so much effort on organizing for social change?

How could we not? Of course, we will never know. But I believe that had we been more actively involved with the communities we served, it might have meant a longer life as an active company.

The Donor

By the time the School got underway our scholarship policy was but one part of a many-pronged effort to make social awareness a core component of our teaching. In 1999 Jennie Kristel, a graduate, had returned for a course called "Teaching Playback Theatre." Impressed by the growth of the School, she asked me if we were organized as a nonprofit. (Jennie would later become a key figure in the introduction of playback theatre to Bangladesh and eventually chair of the School of Playback Theatre board.)

"No," I replied, although I was keenly aware that my brief period of hoping to earn good money from the School had long ago faded into memory.

"With a reorganization," she said, "you could accept donations to help with student scholarships. You could fundraise."

The idea did not sound appealing, until I realized that she was speaking about herself as a donor. What started was a phase of inner debate. I did not take the step lightly, my years of struggle with the nonprofit original company still fresh in my memory. But in the end, I recognized that there was no choice if I were to remain loyal to what I believed. So I said "OK," and called a lawyer.

As a consequence the School of PT became a not-for-profit organization. Funded by Jennie and then others, our rate of scholarships tripled to over 30%. We instituted formal application procedures and made judgment on over fifty scholarship requests per year (up to half our total enrollment). At the same time we began fundraising campaigns, seeking support from both private donors and institutional givers. We called this effort the "Libra Project," which suggested creating balance between those who could find access to training with relative ease and those who could not.

The students who started to appear were not members of a company situated in a wealthy city, pursuing playback as a kind of serious hobby, but pioneers intending to bring this method to whole countries; they were not individuals with disposable time and money seeking personal and professional development, but rather community development officers who saw playback as a way to galvanize and heal communities. Many of us could not even imagine their home context. I remember a Bulgarian explaining that in her country, following the years of communist rule, it was not possible simply to rent a hall for an event, but instead involved permissions, special contacts, and other noneconomic factors. A student from India explained why his playback theatre group performed in an indoor hall only once a year. It took them that long to raise the money for the rental, he said. For their other performances, they would take a bus from the city to an outlying village and perform unannounced outside in the *maidan*. The presence of such colleagues expanded our awareness, and it began to change our concept of playback's applications.

The steady influx of students from a widening geographical region—first Northern Europe, then Japan, South and Southeast Asia, Latin America, and Africa—seemed to have more to do with the word-of-mouth growth of the playback theatre idea than any marketing effort on our part. We spent nothing on advertising, simply announcing each year's program, at first by letter, then later by email and website. Although we stayed committed to our small classes, we often ran three at a time and paradoxically faced the challenge of managing a large group *f*community, all engaged in using personal material as a learning medium. The emotional field often became very dense. But we tempered a focus on skill building with paying attention to the well-being of the group. Even when there were no special problems, we sang together, we argued together, and of course, we did playback theatre together. In this way we avoided many occasions when discomfort, misunderstanding, or injury might spiral out of control, and we had a way, when there was conflict, to deal with it.

My own classes clearly emphasized group communication as well. Our teachers from Australia and New Zealand fit in with this approach: Francis Batten, Bridget Brandon, and their students, like me, had studied psychodrama. However, Francis was also trained in France by Jacques Lecoq, the great French teacher of clown and *commedia*. The Lecoq tradition brought another accent to the work that, while exciting, did not always sit easily with students used to our gentle, creative dramatics approach. It emphasized danger, risk, and being tough before the rigors of the performative moment. A game was more than a game. It taught a kind of combativeness; it taught how to make an improvisational triumph out of the sure prospect of failure. What was most valuable from this teaching was its grounding in improvisational performance, especially since neither I nor Jo had formally studied acting.

Milestone

When the School reorganized as a nonprofit, the budget was $128,000 per year, five times larger than at the start six years earlier. About this time we talked to an expert in "legacy planning" about the school's future. He asked Jo and me what we wanted to get out of the School financially when we retired. We looked at each other. The most we could come up with was "getting our medical insurance paid." The consultant did some reckoning and announced that the school's sustainability, including such a benefit, would require an annual income of $300,000.

I also remember a director of a big-city expressive therapy center saying to me, "Playback is such a great idea. There is no reason your organization should not be as big as mine [$800,000]." It sounded good.

One obvious means was to interest a foundation or other funding source in our work. We hired a consultant and began to reach out to funders. In time it became clear that program officers liked projects rather than trainings; so we started to think of expanding our income stream beyond training.

This period was a decisive one for the School. We could have decided to keep to our summer and winter training sessions and stay at a budget of just over $100,000. After all, Jo and I were the main teachers; we were able to earn enough from the enterprise to get by. But the promise of the playback idea was seductive. Eager students were coming from so many countries. Twenty years after the first forays of the original company, surely by now the time for playback had come. I pictured an office with not three work-stations, but ten. I imagined universities offering degree-granting programs, large organizations committed to using playback, and foundations which would finally want to adopt us.

In 2004, just before the summer session started, we hired Angela Kozlakowski, an administrative assistant with a business background. She was used to a sophisticated work environment. So I was inwardly both appalled and grateful to see her pitching in fully as we lugged sheets and kitchenware into the Vassar student apartments.

Playback now existed in over thirty countries and hundreds of locations without its founders, and the founders' organization, directly benefiting in any way. How could we bring about a shift in this pattern? About this time Jo quit her role as co-director, mainly because she had become fully engaged as the artistic director of Hudson River Playback Theatre, and it was too much for her to manage two nonprofits simultaneously.

Working with Angela, I started programs to bring in new income. We got a technical grant to develop a business plan. Recognizing the School's wider mission, which now included bookings, administrative services, and contracted affiliates, we changed the name of the School once again, this time to the Centre for Playback Theatre. While training continued to be our main focus (151 students attended courses in 2005), we positioned ourselves to become an all-purpose organization devoted to playback theatre and its development. The new administrative demands of the Centre pulled me into the office before eight o'clock every morning. We did not leave our desks for lunch. There was always too much to do. Many of the tasks I found uninspiring, especially the constant search for income. But Angela's encouragement and the lure of playback's growth kept me going.

The devastating Hurricane Katrina in 2005 offered another opportunity for the Centre to expand its services. We coordinated a program that involved establishing a playback theatre company in New Orleans and sending a national performing team to the stricken city six months after the storm. These efforts cost over $20,000, raised mainly from the playback theatre community itself. Two years later we returned to New Orleans to teach a new kind of training under the rubric "PT Responds." It consisted of a training focusing on a special social issue, in this case, the aftermath of natural devastation. The on-site location afforded us many practical advantages, such as learning from community leaders, visiting affected sites, and engaging with community partners. The next year we would mount PT Responds trainings in the Canadian Rockies on climate change and in Plymouth, England, on refugee and immigration issues.

In connection with the New Orleans project we accomplished another milestone. Because those most affected were predominantly black, we did not want to send an all-white team of playback performers to the stricken area. So under the guidance of Pamela Freeman, we organized a workshop called People of Color Working in Playback. Pamela invited me to join, as playback founder and executive director of the Centre. Taking part, I couldn't help remembering my first stumbling social change workshop and noting that here rather than ten to two, the ratio was one to twelve. More important was what I learned.

All the participants belonged to playback companies where they as persons of color were in the minority. Many were the only nonwhite in their group. They lived with a sense of isolation, with misperception, and a feeling of distance from power. "I'm never the conductor," one said. "It's so hard to get access. The leader conducts most of the time. Then there are others in line ahead of me who are more experienced."

Despite my privileged background, I knew beforehand from my experiences in Nepal and elsewhere overseas what it is like to be a minority person in a group. But it was something else again to learn about circumstances in my own profession and in my own country. I really had no idea. Even though there were actually no stories of anger against white playbackers (in part out of kindness to me?), I bore witness to the everyday frustrations of being a non-white playback theatre performer.

In 2007 the theatre department at a branch of the University of California chose to make playback theatre their main semester production and engaged me to teach and take part in the final performances. This work also seemed a harbinger of the future, and we quickly updated our website to market for college residencies.

By 2008 I took the legacy consultant out to lunch, proudly announcing that we had reached the $300,000 mark. It was a moment of great satisfaction. But of course, I was still looking up the road toward $800,000 and beyond.

The Fifth Wall Again

With the paid assistance of a former financial officer of a much larger nonprofit, we submitted a proposal for a federally funded program to create mixed playback teams of college students and community volunteers in cities throughout the United States.

With the help of a university professor, we developed a sixty-page proposal to initiate playback theatre training in the Arab Mideast from another government body, the US Institute of Peace.

Inspired by our work in New Orleans, we set up a course for Europeans called "Emergency Playback," and since the venue was outside Budapest, applied for support to the Trust for Mutual Understanding, a foundation specializing in Russia and Eastern Europe.

We held meetings with a very interested National Library Association to offer PT performances in local libraries throughout the United States, a project that could draw on the many PT groups in North America.

We lobbied the NYS Council on Community Services, a consortium of nonprofits who occasionally hired us, to promote our work to their thousand-strong membership of community organizations.

At the suggestion of a connected friend, we applied to become a registered NGO at the United Nations, thinking it might help us be more recognized.

We even rented a part-time office in NYC in order to be eligible for New York projects that might be funded by community foundations.

In all, we applied to over fifty foundations and potential funding sources.

Not one of these initiatives bore any fruit. Our efforts met with that fifth wall again. We just could not break through.

Funding for any of these projects would have generated work for practicing playbackers and solidified our own position as the central organization for playback theatre in North America and the world. Our hopes of college residencies also failed to generate much activity.

It's not that we had no support. We received a sizable grant for six years from a family foundation that our original donor belonged to. Our bank gave us a small annual donation. But unearned income (grants and donations) never exceeded 17% of the total.

Part of the problem was undercapacity—not enough time for the big stuff, like visiting potential funders as we scrambled to complete the little stuff, such as getting out mailings. Another was undoubtedly my own reticence; it was not easy for me to sell aggressively what was so close to my heart (this is the other side of the coin of Becker's Oedipal Project).

Some of the new initiatives turned out to burden us. For instance, even though we calculated our fees with utmost care, our office staff was too small to carry out the highly detailed demands of fiscal sponsorship work. It drove Angela crazy.

As the first decade of the new century passed its midpoint, we noticed for the first time a decline in enrollment, especially for our second- and third-level core courses. Did we need to offer more fresh courses with sexy titles and certificates at the end? Had we begun to saturate our market? Meanwhile courses on PT and money, PT and youth, PT and men failed to attract enough students despite what had seemed like strong interest.

By now I had been pushing the PT wagon for thirty years.

Even after all this time, we had never found a home in either theatre, psychology, or education. With funders we seemed to meet only rejection. I remained isolated in my upstate office, dreaming big dreams and licking envelopes.

In 2009 Angela, discouraged by our lack of success and worried about the Centre's long-term future, left for another job. The next person I hired did not work out and left after three months. I found myself sitting alone, eyes glued to the computer, trying to decipher financial data and handle the routine chores. Of course this was the year of the collapse of the housing market and the ensuing worldwide recession, eliminating many students' discretionary income. It was in this year also that the Department of Labor decided to audit us, a blow that felt burdensome and unfair.

By the end of the decade, our budget was shrinking. Once again you could find in our filing cabinet numerous five-year financial plans with their goals unrealized. The growth, after a promising start, had stalled. In my constant searching for a new way out, I was sleeping badly, getting up early, staying late at work.

It had happened once again: a beginning characterized by excitement and promise was grinding to an end under a cloud of rejection and failure. In the spring of 2010 I recognized that I had done all I could. With little sense of accomplishment, I packed up my pencils, took my paintings off the wall, and said goodbye to the office.

CHAPTER TWELVE

East, South, West

During my almost twenty years running the theatre school, I kept on traveling the world. The good news was that for the most part my overseas teaching was tied to the School curriculum, which meant that I increasingly taught only the advanced courses, including PT Leadership classes in Japan (in a center close to MOA Museum of Art's Noh Theatre), France (in Heather Robb's theatre center in the land of the Cathars), England (in a fifteenth century monastery), and Germany (in a facility a stone's throw from the old Iron Curtain). There were plenty of other people now to teach beginners. The bad news was that I always felt impelled to stay away as briefly as possible in order to keep up with pressures in the office back home. The result was visiting some marvelous places, but never really stopping to savor them. It felt like a life on the run.

Gradually in my overseas workshops the atmosphere changed. No longer was I facing each time a row of skeptical faces, challenging me to show them something good. The opposite was now true. They were already convinced and many of them regarded me with shining eyes. In the pauses there was scant time to rest anymore. One student needed to tell me of a recent project. Another wanted to talk about a problem in her theatre group. Much of this interest resulted from the increase in playback theatre activity.

But sometimes it went too far. There were the endless photo ops. Some even wanted us to sign their T-shirts. At the core of playback practice rests a kind of deep democracy. Anyone at any time may tell the saving story. Any actor may provide the imaginative impulse in enacting it. We are all equal in our narrative and creative capacity. Lionizing the founders cut against that tenet, causing Jo and me unease.

There was a need for authority, and I was at times criticized for not taking a more interventionist stance in solving problems in faraway playback theatre communities. At one of the early German-speaking gatherings, the organizers, in an effort to help people connect, invited the attendees to collect in groups of about ten each, introduce themselves, then prepare a fluid sculpture-type form to play back a sentiment for all the others. The result looked like a hodge-podge. Yet people definitely enjoyed themselves doing it, and the activity helped build connections. But the next day the leader of a playback theatre company accused me indignantly, saying "How could you let that take place!" I had failed my responsibility as founder to insist on minimal artistic standards on stage, he claimed, for clearly a coherently improvised fluid sculpture is impossible with a group of ten, while I at that moment was just trying to fit in like an ordinary participant.

At the international conferences people's expectations and projections were daunting, especially once the gatherings grew to over three hundred people. Either we were shown off and accorded elevated status by the organizers, which felt uncomfortable, or we were pointedly ignored, which did not work either, since participants seemed to need to see us and honor us. At the conference in 1999 in York, England, so many asked to meet privately with me that in the end I had to set up twenty-minute appointments in what became a nightmare of exhausting exchanges.

I learned at conferences to request to greet everyone in plenary format at the beginning as a means of defusing people's need to meet the founder. In the Frankfurt world conference in 2011 I hit upon a partial solution. At my opening greeting, I said, "I am eager to meet you. Please, as you pass by during the next three days, give me a greeting. Stop and introduce yourself. Or at least wave and say 'Hi.'" The result was surprisingly effective, in a paradoxical way. With explicit permission to stop and talk, many people were content to say, "Hello!" with a laugh as they passed me by. It became a kind of game. Any tension around an encounter with the founder was lifted, and I escaped from a crush of demand.

These complications extended also to the playback process itself. An example: In a performance a teller comes to the chair with me conducting.

"Where does your story take place?" I ask.

"In a playback theatre workshop," says the teller. I am immediately on my guard.

"Who is most important in your story?"

"You are," says the teller.

My worst fears are confirmed. Sometimes I might challenge the teller, or at least ask him if he really wants to tell this story. But usually I simply continue.

"When does it take place?"

"Seven years ago, when you came to our town."

"What's a word to describe you in this story?"

"Hidden, unsure."

"And what's your word for Jonathan in the story?"

"He sees me. He recognizes me."

"Say a little more."

"It was just the way you looked at me. I will never forget it. It was as if all my struggles to be a better actor were validated in that moment, and I was able to do better after that. My confidence was renewed."

I was so empathic, he adds, and came up to him in the break in a gesture of support that he has never forgotten. Needless to say, I don't remember this incident. I even accept the surface truth of it. However, whatever gesture I had made as a person, or even as a teacher that day long ago, is colored by the symbolic significance that has accrued to me as a founding figure.

In the teller's narrative he may well be making an indirect critical statement about his own company director, who may not manifest the positive qualities he has attributed to me. He may be making a statement to his colleagues in the audience: I am special in Jonathan's eyes; he has anointed me. There may also be an element of pure exhibitionism, where the main story is between the teller and his colleagues: Look, I made it to this chair before you did; look at me; Jonathan's conducting my story.

Such stories in a performance are awkward, since they shrink the narrative to a playback story about playback.

Recently a teller took her cellphone out of her pocket as she walked to the chair (to tell a story that had nothing to do with playback or with me, thank goodness). I could see what was coming, and I stopped her. Commemorating the event — telling a story with me as conductor — was taking precedence over the story itself.

In the same vein it has been increasingly difficult for me to be a teller. Of course it is important that I be a teller, not only for my own sake, but to experience what I am asking others to experience. But these founder dynamics make it a dubious practice. Once when I was coaching a European group, they invited me to share one of my own moments, which they enacted in a fluid sculpture. I can no longer remember exactly what my sentiment was. What I do remember very well is that they missed the crux of it. So afterward, when the conductor checked in, I gently said, "Not quite." They were stricken to miss the heart of my story. So they insisted on doing it again. The second time was worse than the first. I demurred after that, saying it was fine, but by now they didn't believe me (rightly), and undertook a third enactment. In the end, of course, they had to stop. But the sense of failure was heavy in the room.

After that, it is a rare occasion when I feel I can let myself tell, even though I am often stirred up by the flow of stories and would be grateful to be a teller.

Maestro, Please!

At the early conferences I was always asked to conduct a performance, and this seemed appropriate, since I was the one who for all practical purposes had invented the playback theatre conductor role. The problem was that I no longer had a company; I wasn't part of a team that practiced together and honed their dramatic power. Playback theatre is so context sensitive and relies so much on ensemble work that to bring in an outsider is always at a cost. The maestro concept might work for an orchestra, but it can be risky for playback theatre — especially when the performing team is not a company.

Once I was asked to run a workshop in Finland. There were 26 participants from various companies. The organizers had set up a performance on the last day without informing me. Again, the main purpose seemed to be to advertise my presence. No careful thought was given to the extra workshop time such a plan necessitated, including the challenge of choosing from among the twenty-six, and the time-consuming task of a technical rehearsal to work out lighting in the lovely but proscenium professional little theatre where the performance was booked. In addition, serious conflict between different groups took time away from focusing on artistic questions. My desperate response to this challenge was to include anyone who wanted to perform in any section of the performance, willingly taking on the looseness that the German playbacker had so irately challenged me about: we had ten for the fluid sculptures, three for the first story, five for the second, and seven for pairs (or something like that).

I did not universally cringe at invitations to be guest conductor. In fact, as I made my transition from stage performer to teacher, I welcomed chances to be in the lights again — when invited by an established company to perform with them, with a decent rehearsal beforehand. It was these pick-up groups at conferences and the need for organizers to feature the founder that I found so problematic.

As time goes by, we have all slowly learned how to manage the conferences, which have steadily grown in size. For example, we now set up the small "home groups," meeting daily with the same people to help offset the sense of being lost in a crowd, and we run many performances concurrently to take away the dangers of an overlarge and unconnected audience. Rewarding as it is, greater diversity presents a range of potential new problems, such as translation (at the 2011 conference in Frankfurt people came from thirty-three countries) and cultural misunderstanding. At contentious moments I have felt heads turn to me as founder, wanting a pronouncement or critique. Naturally at times I have found the work not as good as I had hoped, or reacted negatively to something that someone on stage said or did. But I find the role of public authority distasteful, preferring that we solve problems together.

Hand-written Menu

There came a point when my intro weekends in Japan, hosted by

141

the Research and Consultation Center for Social Growth, became just too frustrating, both for me and for the serious participants, who wanted more. So with the help of Japanese students, especially Kayo Munakata, I opened a branch of the School of Playback Theatre there in 1998. We taught the full range of courses, leading up to graduation. I began a routine of traveling to Japan three times every two years, each time for a two-week stay. As in New York, we invited other internationals to visit while we trained Japanese teachers. Kayo's organizational acumen, combined with the Japanese commitment to education, meant full classes. Kayo is a superb businesswoman. With so much constant worry and penny-pinching at home, it was a kind of liberation to be in Kayo's capable hands on these teaching trips. I also learned a lot. She did not hesitate to take us to eat at a decent restaurant or stay at a comfortable hotel. It was not the culture of poverty I was used to.

It was 1987. I had been to Japan two or three times. The original company had just folded. We were visiting New Zealand for an extended stay (mainly so that our children could get to know their New Zealand family). I decided to look for a Japanese teacher so that I could at least read street signs. (How naive I was, since everywhere street names are among the hardest words of a language to comprehend and decipher). The teacher I found was Vietnamese. I never asked him how he learned Japanese, just as I never asked him why he emigrated to New Zealand. But I imagined a painful, war-driven story. When he started to teach me the rudiments of Japanese writing, especially the Chinese characters, I realized he was a sensei, a true master. You move your hand this way, he said, in a gentle but firm voice. You make the stroke this way. You lift it this way. In my six lessons before we left to return to the United States, I did not get further than a two-stroke sequence. But I had been inspired by the richness of his hidden-away knowledge, his humility, and his gentleness. Twenty-five-odd years later I can read many street signs, but so many more remain inscrutable.

In Japan, one company (Kayo's, not surprisingly) emerged as the most active and engaged with the community. Called Playback-AZ, they are hired by municipalities and airlines, universities and social service organizations. Large stages and microphones do not intimidate them. When I started to introduce the subject of social change in Japan, the members of this group, like the other Japanese practitioners, looked at me befuddled, assuming I was making a cultural mistake. The United States — the rest of the world, perhaps — was crippled by inequality and a past of cruelty and discrimination. But not Japan. I taught a number of workshops on the subject that did not make a splash. But I did not give up.

Slowly the waters started to ripple. In one of these classes a younger person, the youngest there, I think, said, "I don't know if this is true, but I think I remember hearing that there was once a violent clash with some Koreans about water, but I'm really not sure." She was so vague, but we acted it out anyway. As I learned later, after the Kanto earthquake in 1923, Japan's most severe recorded earthquake before the earthquake and tsunami of 2011, false rumors about Koreans poisoning wells led to mob attacks and 231 Koreans killed. No one else there knew the history, or if they did, were willing to speak up about it.

Kayo, who had supported one of her professors at university when he had challenged the government's censoring of accounts of World War II, eventually came to appreciate fully the role of playback theatre in offering a voice to the unheard and their unofficial histories. She also recognized the need of those whose identity had been shaken by traumatic events to carry out what Barbara Myerhoff calls a "definitional ceremony." After the earthquake of 2011 she and the members of Playback-AZ traveled to the Fukushima region. It took them two years of patient community work to obtain the necessary invitation, eventually performing not in a theatre, but an emergency trailer.[15]

The members of Playback-AZ invited me to be their guest conductor for a performance that took place in the Tokyo region. It happened to be the six-month anniversary of the Fukushima tsunami and earthquake. At the rehearsal beforehand, I asked them how best to bring up the subject, or whether it was correct to bring it up at all, knowing that the Japanese are a stoic people. They were surprisingly reticent in their answer. "You decide," was all they would say. I did not know what to make of this. I also felt if I made the wrong choice, the whole performance could fail. I agonized over what to do. In the end, I decided to go ahead, hoping that the playback theatre format would serve as a responsible container for intense community-wide emotion.

When the moment came, the audience seized the opportunity. There was one person there from Fukushima itself. I looked at her directly and asked if she wished to be the teller. She did not hesitate. What we all bore witness to then was a story of great danger, courage, and caring, enacted with requisite power. The Fukushima teller's story and the short enactments that came before it provided a hard-to-find catharsis of a deeply felt social crisis. After the performance the mood was ebullient. I did not mind then posing for photos and signing autographs, because I knew my presence had helped catalyze a community's need for a definitional ceremony.

On an earlier trip Jo and I together went to Hiroshima. The story one encounters in the museum there is overwhelming. But at least it is situated in the midst of a park, allowing one to walk in and walk out through nature. The city does not need pointers on the importance of never forgetting, and it has partnered with playback theatre practitioners to stage performances there. But playback has never taken off in Hiroshima. One reason is the lack of interest of younger generations, for whom the compulsory school field trip to the Peace Museum is exposure enough.

One of Kayo's children, Akiko Komori, was a teen when her mother got so involved in playback. Like Hannah, Akiko took a strong interest herself as she completed school and university, eventually joining Playback-AZ and becoming a faculty member of the Japan School of PT. She now has three children, including twin girls. At the post-graduation party a couple of years ago I approached a circle of women ooh'ing and ah'ing over this pair of 3-month old babies. As I approached, Kaho-chan reached out for me, then Mayu-chan did. As I held them, my heart suddenly dissolved, and I did not want to let them go. When first Maddy, then Hannah had their own boys not long after, I was ready to be a grandfather from the first day.

To work in Japan was rewarding in many ways, including my familiarity with Asia from my time in Nepal, prior reading about Japanese theatre, and an attraction to the paradoxes of imperfection and emptiness in Zen. I am recalling a dinner in a ryokan, a traditional inn, the kind with shoji screens for windows and futons unrolled on the tatami mat floor. One eats in one's room with one's friends, dressed in robes after soaking in a hot spring. It is a long meal with many courses, brought by a server who kneels in a ritual bow each time. There is a menu to refer to as the dishes are brought out. I cannot read this menu. But I see it is written by hand, and I know it is written by the chef. The bustling preparation of this repast is invisible, nor are we privy to the planning and consideration of each dish. The chef is not to be seen. But he shows himself in the menu, in the grace of his calligraphy.

In playback theatre, to be sure, there is no menu—no text, nothing that will remain as a testament when the meal is done. But there is something about the style of this custom, with its bow to aesthetic expression, ceremony, and service, that appeals to my playback mind and underlies my gratitude to the people and culture of Japan.

An Unfinished Story

I was excited to be taking the long trip back to Africa, where I would be encountering a culture so far from my own. Would there again be a positive meeting between two forms of the oral tradition, old and new?

On my first trip, just after the 9/11 terrorist attacks, when everyone was urging me to cancel, the director of Search for Common Ground's Burundi program, a man named Louis, insisted on three days of socializing before I started my teaching. I attended a party with my students. We went walking together. We ate meals, provided by the NGO. We drank beer. Louis was simpatico, and he understood the importance of taking time to connect. When I admitted to him, looking at the days ahead and my task of training newcomers for performances in a very short time, that I was not sure I could pull it off—I meant it, knowing the combination of factors, contextual and personal, that would be necessary for them to achieve effective playback theatre performances—he replied: "It's already a success." Louis's confidence helped me a lot. He meant, I think, that he saw I was interested in the students as persons, and for him, that quality of mutual regard was key. I felt in the right place at the right time — even though I listened with trepidation to the sound of guns firing outside the curfewed city.

Now we are in Ngozi, Burundi, not far from the Rwandan border. It is 2003. The United States has just attacked Iraq, and I am very upset. But it is only alone in my room at night that I have time to dwell on it, as my thoughts meld the war now taking place in the Middle East and the ethnic killings that took place here and throughout this verdant, hilly land. We are about to start our last full day of work. The workspace consists of a cement block room, with openings to let in the daylight. But from the first day on, these "windows" have been darkened by faces peering in, and the room is enveloped in its own penumbral light. The group is in good spirits. They have worked hard, performed playback theatre for four different audiences, and on the whole, brought it off.

Three days earlier one of the group told a long-bottled-up story about the death of his mother. He recounted in detail his coming home from elementary school to find her no longer alive (the death did not seem to be caused by war violence). The performers played back Baptiste's tale with a fluid sculpture — in other words, they ignored the plot completely and showed only a modicum of the feeling. It was a standard response from actors afraid to hear a story. The next day, in a different context, he told the same story again. How could one blame him? For he had failed to see the first time what he needed to see. The second conductor in the second performance, not knowing what had happened the previous day, did the same thing: "Let's see this in a fluid sculpture" (unbelievably).

Now we are almost at the end of the workshop. It is a teachable moment, and when I ask Baptiste if under my guidance he would like to finally see his story, he enthusiastically assents.

The conditions are far from optimal. To revisit a big story on the last day will shorten the time for closure, even while it increases the need for it. There is a language issue: the teller's Kirundi will have to be translated into French for a conductor whose thoughts run in English, increasing the level of risk. But it feels worse to let Baptiste's story hang unfinished.

So we do it. I conduct. This time the actors who step forward know they will be expected to enact a full story, and in fact they do an excellent job, showing a carefree boy walking home, his shocking discovery, his heartbreak. From his nods and demeanor afterward, Baptiste finds at last the release he has been seeking. He is sad, yet satisfied to see the details of his story on the stage.

For many in the audience, however, the enactment triggers their own untold trauma. Some start to weep as soon as the words "death of my mother" are spoken. Others cannot even stay in the room and rush away. Have I done the right thing to specially evoke this story?

Mainly as a support for the witnesses, I invite Baptiste to re-member a happy moment with his mother, and we play that back. And we follow that transformation scene with a series of short forms, reflecting a range of responses from the audience (one young man said, "I don't feel anything anymore, including now.")

"We need to cry," said a civic leader whom I later consulted. Indeed, it seemed so many in this deceptively peaceful land had not yet had the right space, the safety, and the right ritual structure to cry.

Unfortunately, Search for Common Ground, the conflict res-olution NGO sponsoring our work, sought quicker and more tangible results than we could produce. Search was unwilling to expend the resources for a full-fledged playback training, let alone the education in emotional resilience that I felt needed to go with it.

It was a great pleasure for me to walk on the dusty roads of Ngozi (we were told that Karin Gisler, my co-leader, and I were the first white people that they had ever seen walking like them instead of speeding by in a jeep); to meander through the great market of Bujumbura; to drink a beer outside chatting as the dusk deepened. I felt there was hope in Africa for our way of storytell-ing, of remembering, of reaching for a life-sustaining tale.

Meanwhile as the years progressed, playback theatre emerged in other African locations. People in Cameroon, Botswana, Angola, South Africa, and Egypt made their own discovery of playback theatre and started to use it for their own distinctive ends. Perhaps this is the best form of transmission, as opposed to a top-down, NGO-funded approach that looks similar to the old colonial ways.

Looking back, it seems the span of my working life has been but the length of a day, and I am riding my own sun's arc toward evening. Will I ever return to Africa?

Praise Be

In 2008 the University of Kassel held a one-day symposium about playback theatre. The jaws of the playback practitioners in the audience, about a hundred, dropped to hear talks such as "Playback Theatre from the Vantage Point of Consciousness Research" and "Playbacktheater und Psychoanalyse." They were not used to hearing learned intellects appreciating their work.

The occasion was a very personal one. Over the years my hopes for a playback breakthrough had risen so many times, only to be squashed, that when Heinrich Dauber phoned me in 2006 to ask if I would allow him to put my name forward for an honorary doctorate at his university, my reaction was distinctly mixed. Here we go, I thought. The first step was not too difficult—preparing a CV, publications list, and so forth. The second step was more challenging—showing up in Kassel to speak informally to a roomful of department heads. The third step was downright intimidating—addressing the faculty. The *Gesamthochschule* obviously took these kinds of decisions very seriously. The department of education and humanities had previously awarded honorary degrees to only five individuals. Following the faculty talk, the entire faculty senate and various officials, including the president, needed to vote and sign off on the award. In the process Heinrich had also obtained approval for awarding the doctorate for both artistic and scholarly achievement, a singular honor.

As the months of deliberation in Germany went by, I tried not to think about it. But by this time, despite myself, I had begun to hope.

To my delight and surprise, Kassel said Yes. Those hundred playbackers, along with Jo and university faculty, had come for the investiture. In addition to the symposium, there was a lovely ceremony with superb music. During the *Laudatio*, Heinrich not only projected a photo of me as I looked back in the 1970s, with over-sized head of hair and bib overalls, but also presented me with a copy of my grandfather Elias's PhD dissertation, which he had unearthed in Munich. When I stood to receive the diploma happiness filled me, and before speaking I did a Nelson Mandela-inspired dance of joy. Everyone started clapping in unison, and by the end the very formal dean who had presented the diploma was himself flushed with feeling and actually gave me a hug.

The ceremony took place in one of the university's prime meeting halls, a place I knew as one of the only structures to survive the Allied bombing of Kassel in World War II, despite the fact that it had been used as a foundry for making German trains, transporters of so many Jews and others to oblivion.

Because since its inception playback theatre has been widely considered neither artistically nor academically relevant (no text, no repeated action, no literary antecedents), it was a particular pleasure to receive an award for both an artistic and a scholarly contribution, and I rejoiced to see academics putting their intellectual muscle to investigate questions raised by our practice. Their attention was a kind of recognition and a sign that playback theatre has been edging toward the mainstream.

At least articles about playback theatre are no longer confined to our own newsletters. In theatre publications you can find "A New Paradigm of Popular Play: Playback as Bakhtinian Novelistic Theatre," "Audiencing the Audience: Playback Theatre, Performative Writing, and Social Activism," and "Playback Theatre: Inciting Dialogue and Building Community through Personal Story" (the last one written by our daughter, Hannah).

Outside the theatre field, the journal *Organizational Studies* published a paper titled "The Politics of Performance in Organizational Theatre-Based Training and Interventions." The book *Building Nations: Transitional Justice in the African Great Lakes Region* mentions playback theatre, as does the journal *Reflexivity* in an article titled "Navigating Multiple Research Identities: Reflexivity in Discourse Analytic Research." You can find "Playback Theatre: Effects on Students' Views of Aggression and Empathy Within a Forensic Context," "Playback Theatre as a Tool to Enhance Communication in Medical Education," and "Quakerism and the Arts: An Experiment with Drama and Religion," as well as scores of others, including the doctoral dissertation of our daughter, Maddy, "The Knowing Body: Participatory Artistic-Embodied Methodologies for Re-Imagining Adolescence."

Bakhtinian Theatre and Consciousness Research, Reflexivity and Quakerism. They describe a method that is a far cry from the original stripped-down vision of an empty stage, ready actors, and the stories of ordinary folk. But my pride at this flowering of scholarship does not replace the commitment I still feel for the basic idea. On a recent trip to the West Indies, a professor took me to her evening class of teachers-in-training. There was no way for her to advise them ahead of time that she was bringing a guest (let alone the founder of a worldwide movement). She had charged me with the assignment of introducing them to playback theatre, even though they had no evident interest in the subject. I needed to work hard not to threaten them with too much physical work, too much drama. But by the end, they had shared a couple of very rich stories, and even acted them out. They were talking excitedly. The teacher was also excited. Once again, we had started from zero, and their stories had elevated them to a state of animation.

On that same trip a newly enthused young woman came up to me at the end of the day to invite me to her country, Guyana. I was touched. Was there anywhere playback theatre would not eventually reach? But it most likely would not be I who would one day teach there. I felt the bittersweet sensation of missing people I had not met, those bright-faced Guyanese, discovering a new kind of creativity through enacting each others' stories.

CHAPTER THIRTEEN

Handful of Cherries

It is a strange irony, how one's dream may come true beyond one's imagining, and at the same time to have a sense of failure. When I started this memoir, I had a sharp sense of having fallen short. Struggling up the cobblestone street pulling my heavy cart, slipping on the wet stones, ready to drop at any moment. The voices of my critics pounding in my ears. That fifth wall was thick indeed. I just did not have the smarts and the strength to break through. My self-absorption had its zenith in a waking fantasy, in which all the charges were levied against me.

I found myself in a dark and hollow building. Gigantic. The feeble, eerie light did not permit much visual information, but I could tell I was high up, close to the top, standing on a walkway that hugged the inside wall. It sloped downward. There seemed to be nothing in the vast interior. It was hard to discern how high up we were, but my senses told me we were at least six stories. What kind of a building was this? And what was I doing there?

"We've been waiting for you," intoned a cold male voice. "Not everyone has been happy."

My mind raced. Not happy with what?

"Look to your right," the voice said. I looked and saw a familiar sight: embedded in the wall was a diorama of a playback theatre story in the process of enactment. I saw the conductor sitting with the teller. I saw the actors in a frozen pose on stage. I saw a musician playing an instrument. The scene was breathtakingly realistic. It did everything but move.

What was a playback theatre exhibit doing here? "This is the subject of your interrogation," said the voice. Then it repeated:

151

"Not everyone is happy."

Suddenly claustrophobic, I turned to leave, but I saw only blackness. The voice cackled. "Don't even think of it. Just walk forward and answer the questions."

What did I do to deserve this, I thought indignantly. But I have to admit, I was also a bit intrigued.

"Walk!" said the voice.

Balking, I turned to my left and looked over the not very high railing. I could see exhibits along the exterior as the path descended, with nothing but a vast space in the center. At the bottom, set in a warm light, ranged a series of lounge chairs with people reclining on them. They looked comfortable indeed. But a long way away.

"Walk!"

I walked forward slowly, looking to my right, as I had been instructed to do. I felt very alone.

Passing beyond the first diorama, I came to a large photo of my stepfather with my mother in the background. He was staring straight at me. "You did not live up to our expectation of you," he said. "We thought you would make us proud. Why go to Harvard if you were going to end up as you did, doing knee bends and making stupid noises? All the money spent. All the education wasted."

My feelings were so mixed. I felt shock and some sadness at experiencing this combination of their images and voices, sprung, as it were, from the dead. I wanted to hang my head. But I also wanted to defend myself.

"That was not a world I..."

"Walk!" said the disembodied voice. I was puzzled. Wasn't I supposed to answer?

Answering, however, was not easy. How was one to defend a life? So I merely shrugged and went onward, continuing on to the next panels. Every exhibit was a little different in its design, but with each one, a charge was levied. Some of them contradicted each other.

"This theatre you have devoted yourself to so ardently is little more than the game of charades," accused one figure wearing a coat and tie. "Not to be considered in the ranks of serious endeavors. Mere play."

"You use this word 'theatre,' but you have no proper training in theatre. You are a fly-by-night, unlike your father, who at least was a legitimate actor."

My father! I thought. My father, who told me never to get involved in theatre. I pictured him in one of his major roles, Tybalt in *Romeo and Juliet*, with sword in hand. Help me now! I wished.

I came to another set of stern faces, also very bourgeois-looking: "Whatever this psychodrama is, you dove into it. Yet you keep mum about its hold on you."

"You have tried to fashion a form of therapy," said another.

"Yes, but a two-bit pseudotherapy!" said another.

In a small window, I saw myself sitting at my desk. The disembodied voice spoke: "Look at this. The phone is idle. You are sitting cozy in your little office rather than building contacts. You were never a true institution-builder."

No sooner had I stammered out the beginning of an answer when the voice interrupted.

"There is frequent conflict in these national movements of yours, but you stand back. You are no true guru!"

"Did I ever say I was?" I cried.

"Yet you have created a cult," I heard, as I approached yet another panel, which showed a photo of a group of smiling, joyous people. "See all your devotees, so eager for their spiritual titillation?"

"You are no true artist," charged the figures in another panel, who seemed to be on a rehearsal stage with texts in hand. "The inferior work you have let transpire before your eyes, never interrupting, never condemning—shameful! You didn't have the courage to enforce allegiance to the forms that you created."

Suddenly there was my father again. Not in costume, but in his familiar blue cardigan. "You have to admit," he said, "not everyone's story is interesting. So many people live dull lives. You just can't take on acting out whatever they have to tell. It's just too dull."

Yearning to be finished, to reach the lounge chairs on the ground floor—what happens there? what is the reward? I wondered—I found myself suddenly back at my real desk, memoir staring out of the screen before me.

I had stood accused, and in fact, much of it was true.

Parade of Marvels

Pretty grim, eh? Well, I have to admit that a part of my overall experience was to struggle. Perhaps it is a founder's syndrome. It is often those who follow who triumph, for example, while the discoverer never quite comes up with the breakthrough. Yes, some of this may be at play. At the same time I know that many PT practitioners have gone/are going through their own struggles. No theatre enterprise is easy, for a start. That playback theatre transgresses conventional categories makes it even harder to succeed with it. Especially playback's dance around the distinction between the market and gift economy, our blending of avocation and vocation, is likely to put you in a situation where you wake up one morning to find yourself in an office in an empty warehouse with no heat. Or entering a hall to find that you have to move chairs yourself to create a performance space.

But it has not all been struggle. Not by a long shot. Otherwise I would not have wanted to continue. By now I feel that that fantasy of mine is very self-absorbed. The focus is all on me—the inverse, perhaps, of my stepfather's dictum of "being number one." But the development and growth of playback theatre was not all *me*, nor even me and Jo. It was *us*, all of us slowly spreading from town to town, continent to continent. A collaboration that started as soon as I rushed home and told Jo about my new idea, and continues to this day.

This collective creation involved the original company, those brave experimenters willing to blindly follow a fast-talking long-haired man. The new companies, undaunted by a form with no clear models, which emerged in Australia, New Zealand, Europe, Japan. The groups that grew up in cities throughout the world, including Asia, Latin America, Africa, the Middle East. Whatever was accomplished, we all did together.

When I look back I see a parade of people, initially students, later colleagues, who brought great enthusiasm and creativity to the work. Some of them I have named in these pages, but most I have not, since there are so many of them and my aim has been not to write a history, but simply to tell my own story in it.

ee cummings, to whom I devoted a major essay in high school, wrote about unforgettable people he met, who stayed in his heart because of their transcendent quality. He called them Delectable Mountains.[16] The name is a bit odd. Perhaps it is best not to give them a collective name, for a marvelous encounter for me might be ordinary for you, and vice versa. Furthermore in a sense that cummings was hinting at and I find compatible, we are all transcendent souls.

I remember Leon, the camp director who took a lonely kid out for morning bird walks in the woods and showed him how to listen.

That sadhvi in Nepal, the interloper on my verandah, who patiently waited for just the right moment to touch my heart.

My first Japanese-language teacher, the one who taught me to write the number one and the number ten and in what seemed like a mere flick of the wrist opened the doorway to the traditional arts.

Judy, our long-time colleague and friend, for whom every person seems to be a marvel.

The two Dominican sisters at Falling Waters, our site for course retreats, who despite advancing age, cook day after day with open hearts.

Each one is a crystal, shining in the light. Each one a collection of stories. If the person as well as the pismire is equally perfect, then we must treat everyone as precious, including ourselves. No, the project did not fail.

Tales to Live By

Once at a party in the summer resort of Easthampton I met the renowned British sculpture Henry Moore. Giving advice to an impressionable youth, he told me that his aim was to carve his life as he would a sculpture.

An inspiring example came from my grandmother, Dora. Late in her life we were sitting in the sunroom of a rehabilitation facility, where she was recuperating from a hospital stay. I remember what she told me that day not only because of the subject matter—sex was one topic—but also because of her vitality and joy in telling me what was precious to her. I admired her decision to make of that moment what she did, when it would have been easy to give in to the fatigue and depression of being ill.

When we performed in New Orleans after Hurricane Katrina a woman told a story about the gutting of her house. Everything had to be removed and destroyed because of water damage. But the family piano, which had come down to her, she refused to let them take away, even though it was also ruined. The bare wooden frame of the house was left with a grand piano sitting in the middle. Nature had devastated this family and their possessions, but the teller would not let fate have the last word. She carved her own story, and insisted on an ending that included the piano.

From the start we welcomed any story, even the most ordinary, striving to give it aesthetic meaning. But even beyond that challenge, there is value in what Adrienne Rich calls "prose-bound routine remembering" as a kind of warm-up or practice for the sharing of the big stories, the stories not so easy either to tell or to hear. So many stories have stayed with me because, like good literature, they held lessons for life: the woman who got lost on the way to see a new therapist; the soldier walking past the road sign marker in Vietnam.

Others are unforgettable because they recount life-shattering moments: the son of the hog butcher cutting himself with his father's slaughtering knife, the Burundian boy coming home from school to discover his dead mother. The accidents, the deaths, the moments of great hardship—some a natural part of life, even if often unspoken; others expanding our sense of what human life means.

These stories were an education for me of a kind I did not get in school, such as the Japanese woman's story about visiting Seoul and learning about the sex tourism there. In this case it was not the teller's point of view that touched me—in fact, she kept to herself what she thought about it all—but the events themselves, which I had never considered, especially as I learned more about the complex and painful history of Korea and Japan.

Some stories are very hard to tell. Once a Japanese woman of Korean background came all the way to New York to a one-day training of ours because she felt her story could not be told in her country, as did a German woman, child of Nazis, who could only tell what she needed to tell far from her native land.[17]

Such stories sparked an interest in history. The story of the French schoolboy silenced in music class spurred me to read more about the treatment of Jews in France, leading me to imagine vividly the contrast between the boy's home life, enveloped in anguish as news of the Holocaust emerged, and a harsh, even hostile atmosphere in school. Later I discovered from follow-up discussion with the teller that he was not mistreated; he even received prizes. This knowledge in turn led me to reflect on how I received that story and the contrast between my imagination of the boy's circumstance in school and my own classroom at roughly the same time. In the US there was an atmosphere of omnipotence following the dropping of the A-bomb and the American victory on all fronts of the war. It never sat easy with me, this proud stance, and I would have reached out eagerly to my unknown peer in France.

Many stories inspired. I think of a Finnish teller at one of the regional playback conferences in Helsinki, who began his account with the sentence, "I want to tell you all why I am here today." He then went on to relate a story about a terrible auto accident he had suffered while driving from the north to the capital on his birthday. During his long recuperation in hospital and once back in his everyday life, he despaired of ever regaining his former joie de vivre, of experiencing that birthday party, as it were, that he forever missed. Until he met playback theatre and found a new outlet for his energy and creativity. To my eyes sitting in the audience that day, the actors missed the mark because they emphasized in the enactment the gruesome details of the accident and his long, difficult recovery. But the main point was the "why I am here today," the surviving of an ordeal and coming to the other side.

In New Orleans during the same church performance where one teller after another told of their traumas from Hurricane Katrina, the last teller was a man who ambled to the front and said, "I don't really have a story." He went on:

I came here to the church this morning for a funeral. Afterward I was going to head back to where I'm staying, when I saw there was a wedding about to take place. So I ended up staying for that. After that I was once again heading home, but then I heard there was going to be a theatre performance. So once more I ended up staying. And here I am. I meant to go home this morning, but I'm still here and now it is evening.

Here was a "nonstory." Yet it expressed a kind of answer to the ones before. It had the power to lift us up with its message, telling the New Orleans congregation that no matter that we may be alone, no matter that we may be dealing with upheaval and grief, no matter that we are in temporary housing and in difficult daily circumstances, the church is here for us. We can remain in the church. It will welcome us and see us through the day. It was a story to give one hope.

The few professional and many, many community playback theatre groups devoted to embodying all these stories, those I have met and worked with and the many that I have not, are themselves a rich and marvelous story. The group from Northern Europe who call themselves "Big Men" when performing at conferences. The queer PT groups. The German group specializing in inviting stories about cancer called the Tumorists (the performers all are living with or have lived with cancer). The group in England consisting of black women called Breathing Fire. The company of deaf performers in Brazil. The Swiss group of elderly called Vi-echo, punning on "echo," as in "play back," and "viejo," the Spanish for "old." The group in Japan of young mothers devoted to enacting the experiences of other young mothers.

Stories have provided me guidance for living, especially as recounted in a playback context infused with warmth and respect for persons. They have reminded me that life is precious. As Barbara Myerhoff, the anthropologist who increasingly left science behind in favor of storytelling, says, "And that is what we mean when we say that a life matters: that it has come from someplace and it goes to someplace. And thereby a mending, a kind of fundamental healing takes place when a story is being told and heard."[18]

Healing Places

Nadia Lotti and Luca Verri live on a protected site in the pre-Alps, where Nadia runs a training center for ecological awareness. Snow-capped mountains are visible in most directions. Their house is midway between the valley floor and a ridge. They manage to grow a great deal of their food, and trade for more. There is a special feeling to the place, which is called Lunalpina. One could imagine oneself halfway to heaven.

I have held workshops there, in the former schoolhouse the local village allowed Nadia to renovate for a training space. It is not only being in the company of Nadia, Luca, and their family that is a joy. It is also being at Lunalpina.

That is also true about the hall beside the sea at Paekakariki in New Zealand, with magical Kapiti Island across the water. Heather Robb's hilltop villa in southern France, with its ancient-walled theatre. The Daishin-In temple in Kyoto, surrounded by its Zen garden. The renovated monastery at Buckden in rural England, once residence of Catherine of Aragon and now home to the oldest plane tree in the United Kingdom. Falling Waters, site of the Centre's winter sessions, looking out over the majestic Hudson River. And even the funky Unison Arts Center, surrounded by woods, where we held our first trainings.

There is something about these places of sanctuary that soothes the soul. We all have our own special spots. It might be a favorite beach, or our garden, or that corner of our home, where the sun comes in just so. Being in such places gives us a sense of wholeness. It would seem that being close to nature is important to this feeling.[19]

When I started out, I wanted to liberate our theatre from the confines of traditional theatre. I was an evangelist for community locations. But not just anywhere will do, we learned. A nondescript room in a nondescript building with no view and an industrial rug or linoleum on the floor presented an obstacle to our aims. The warm light that stood out in my original vision translated into insisting that the audience be always visible (to us and to each other) and that the performers be lit invitingly. We wanted windows, too, ideally that allowed a view of trees and sky. The spectator seats needed to be arranged so that audience members could see each other and be able to walk to the stage to take the teller's chair. The performers wore attractive but neutral clothing.

I have a wonderful recurring dream. It is not what happens in it, or who appears, that fills me with joy, but where it takes place. I am visiting an island in Maine, sometimes many islands. The air is always soft, the foliage verdant. The beach glitters with colored stones, the wave crests shine in the sunlight. After one of these dreams, I invariably wake up with a light and joyful heart.

We aimed to shape the playback theatre experience in such a way that the participants emerged afterward with a light and joyful heart — not because we avoided stories of suffering and the difficulties of life, to the contrary — but because the ceremony, set in a benign and pleasant place, took them to the other side of it. It took them beyond.

Can I Play?

My grandfather, the scholar who obtained his PhD in Germany, was given a memorial ceremony at All Soul's College, Oxford, after his death, but I know nothing about the funerals of my other grandparents. My other grandfather died before I was born, so there is an excuse, perhaps, for that one. But my grandmothers, both of them, were relegated to the earth so unceremoniously that I have no memory of what happened. I did not question these practices at the time. It seems that traditions of mourning, like so much else, were left behind while getting ahead in America.

Asia, especially Japan, showed me a different way to live. At a Kyoto temple, for instance, or in an authentic tea ceremony, repetitive practices provided a container for holding emotion. You drink the water just so. You sit just so. You turn the cup three times just so, appreciating its beauty. Our experiences in New Zealand also exposed us to the rhetoric and rituals of public Maori ceremonial events.

What we learned informed how we created a container for the improvisational freedom of playback theatre, a structure that included inviting the teller always to sit in the same chair, asking her the same series of questions, saying at the right moment, "Let's watch!" and then dismissing her when the tale was finished and she had spoken her last word.

And the actors listened just so; and when they had completed their enactment, they stood and looked at the teller just so. We learned from practice that when we could do it right, this ritual held great power. Learning the skill, conceptually and practically, was a many-year journey, made much more challenging because we needed to invent it. I recall that when my first Japanese teacher came to give me a lesson, I instructed Maddy, then about ten, to bring tea on a tray and retreat without turning her back to the master; my instructions were given in a playful spirit, and she joined in the game, but by then I knew it was more than a game.

We learned that our performances and workshops contained a kind of ceremony that followed its own rhythm. The stronger the emotion, the more important to keep to the structure. The presence of the ritual helped a woman tell about her house fire, and another about the violent outbursts of her elderly mother, and know that neither they nor those on stage would be overwhelmed. Once while introducing playback theatre as a guest teacher at an eastern US university graduate department, I learned that one member of the class was a Native American from a western reservation. I wondered if he had been invited to tell his story, and after lunch I asked him. By his answer, it seemed clear that no one had shown any interest in his unique background (or perhaps they were too shy to ask). So I invited him to be a teller. He responded without hesitation. That I had noticed him may have played some part in his decision, but more important, I am sure, was his sense that even though playback theatre was improvisation, its ritual held story and teller with even-handed care and respect.

When the ritual cannot be adhered to, then the performance becomes ethically questionable because a key source of safety will be missing. When we visited the site of our New Orleans church performance and saw the layout, we were filled with concern. On one side of the chancel stood a large piano; on the other, an organ; in between was a podium that could not be moved. There was no place for the teller's and conductor's chairs and no place for a stage—essential spatial elements of the ritual. We looked around the building for a possible alternative playing space, but there was none. What to do? Cancel the performance, after so much painstaking preparation? We decided to perform in front of the chancel in the area between it and the pews. The teller and conductor would have to stand facing the audience for the interview, then sit in the front row to watch the enactment. This was a very big departure from our traditional set-up, which has the teller visible at all times.

There was another problem. We had no musician, and music is so key a component of both the art and ritual of what we do. So we asked the pastor if there was perhaps a musician in the congregation who would be willing to help us out. After all, this was New Orleans. He promised us a volunteer. As it turned out, we got our man, an elderly parishioner, only ten minutes before the show. There was no time to rehearse with him, or even hear what he could do. Not performing myself that day, I sat next to him up at the organ. I told him I would tell him when to play. I noticed very soon that he played in a gospel style that lacked the flexibility that playback needs. So when he asked me, "Now?" I often found myself saying, "Wait." It became more and more awkward, for the more he said, "Now?" the more I said "Wait!"

There was a climactic moment when a woman decided to tell of the family loss that she had not been able to put words to before that day. She stood before the assembled audience, with Pamela the conductor at her side, and told her story. Even now she had trouble getting it out, and her husband came up to stand beside her. She told about a desperate ride around the city in a truck to collect family members, but failing to get them all, then having to escape the flood, fearing the worst for those missing. Later she learned that two had died.

Then the woman and Pamela sat down in the front row of the audience while the performers acted out the story. In a typical performance the audience would see the teller watching the enactment and be a witness to her response during and after. But this time they could not see her. It took a long time for her to become composed. I could feel audience members, so many themselves undoubtedly suffering their own losses, sinking into a hole of despair.

"Now?" asked the old man, whom I had forgotten about as I watched with dismay what was unfolding. "Yes, now!" I responded. What emerged from the musician's fingers and voice that afternoon was as if from the beyond. He turned out to be a great blues singer. He knew the woman and the congregation as well. You could feel the hearts easing, the breaths deepening as he sang. He played one number, then another, then a third, each one speaking directly to his people. And he rescued the situation.

It was after this moment that the man came forward with the "nonstory" about coming to services that morning and never leaving, who told the transformative story of a healing community. But it was the old musician who made it possible by sewing up the fabric of our ruptured ritual.

Textlessness

We have received many gifts over the years, but they are simple: straw placemats from India, a candle holder from Africa, a pine cone from Siberia—humble offerings, not unlike the handful of cherries in the Second Shepherd's Play.

Most important has been the exchange at the core of Jo's and my work. We gave our idea, our dedication, our teaching, at times even our extra bed, and received in return respect and gratitude. We were also fortunate in being able to make playback theatre our vocation as well as avocation.

So many playbackers perform as volunteers, giving their time and their expertise in exchange for people's stories.

As did the old New Orleans musician, who gave his songs in exchange for a precious moment to sing them.

Judy Swallow gave me a book by a philosopher named Paul Woodruff called *Reverence*. I did not look at it right away. Finally I started it, but put it down. It was only many years later that I picked it up again and this time read it through. Reverence, according to Woodruff, is a virtue. It demands respect, awe, and a sense of your own imperfection.[20]

In Japan a gray-haired psychology professor came to my courses. Despite his rank—everyone called him Sugitani-sensei—he behaved in class like any other student. He was a devotee of

Noh, and once in a private moment he brought out his text and introduced me to the extremely difficult but fascinating mystery of Noh recitation. I was grateful for our sense of joy singing together, despite our difference in age and culture. Years later I was only half surprised to receive an invitation to a public exhibit of his calligraphy. How grand his scrolls were, how beautiful.

Sugitani-sensei understood about reverence. Despite his status, he did not hesitate to study Noh, practice calligraphy, and even be a beginner in learning something so nontraditional as playback theatre.

I think of all the tellers who followed an unfamiliar urge and came to the teller's chair. And all those who let their story surprise them.

The performers who exclaim how much they love playback theatre make me uneasy when their tone does not also convey a sense of the long path.

Playback theatre practice demands reverence, and the practitioners closest to my heart will never rest easy no matter how deep their experience because there is always something more — to learn, to teach, to guide, to give.

One of my aunts came to an early performance. A woman who spoke her mind, she stood up mid-show and directly criticized what we were doing. What a spontaneity test for me as conductor! Many people have come to playback theatre, and, if more politely, reacted in a similar way. Playback theatre's simplicity, its rough and holy nature, its variability, and its textlessness irritated their critical mind. (I accepted my aunt's critique, and then surprised her with a "Let's watch," sending her sentiment to the actors.)

I have put my best intellect to what we were doing, of course, and worked hard to become a better artist and teacher. But at bottom what has mattered more was the invitation to participate with an open heart. It was in this spirit that I announced at our first meeting a program of free community performances. It was in this spirit we traveled to New Orleans to enact the stories of the storm.

This is the only way to oneness, that transcendent state that I felt at that outdoor concert as a child and which the playback theatre event can occasionally accomplish for its participants, including myself, whether I am onstage or in the audience.

I was never fully consistent. I yearned for mainstream success. But it was the taste of another kind of food that kept me going. Of the kind we savored at the performance where the father told about fishing with his young son. Of the kind told by a young man named Francis about his struggle to keep dancing. Of the kind where a wooden camel spitting insults could fill adults with child-like glee.

It is not a question of accomplishment. Or what problems we have solved. Or whether it is actually theatre or not. But rather the richness and wonder of people's lives, our connections, and the flow of our stories. We have sought a certain kind of music. Teilhard de Chardin called it the Omega point. Martin Luther King, Jr. called it the Beloved Community. The medium has been a theatrical ceremony designed to create an atmosphere, a resonance, assuring us that we are not alone, that our life has a worth, and that we are an integral part of the living universe.

Notes

1 Defined by Jan Cohen-Cruz as "a field in which artists, collaborating with people whose lives directly inform the subject matter, express collective meaning." See her *Local Acts: Community-based Performance in the United States* (Rutgers University Press, 2005), p. 1.

2 For appreciation of psychodrama as *theatre*, see the critic Eric Bentley's references to psychodrama in *Theatre of War* (Viking, 1972), and "Magister Ludi," an unpublished essay by sociodramatist and playback colleague Francis Batten.

3 See the BBC Omnibus film about Dorothy Heathcote, *Three Looms Waiting* (1971) and John Heilpern, *Conference of the Birds: The Story of Peter Brook in Africa* (Faber & Faber, 1977).

4 See Simon Palfrey and Tiffany Stern, *Shakespeare in Parts* (Oxford University Press, 2011).

5 See James C. Kaufman, et al. "Creativity Polymathy: What Benjamin Franklin Can Teach Your Kindergartener," *Learning & Individual Differences*, 20, 380-387, and Paul Woodruff, *The Necessity of Theater* (Oxford University Press, 2008).

6 Jo Salas refers to this event in *Improvising Real Life: Personal Story in Playback Theatre*, p. 107.

7 *Gathering Voices* (Tusitala Publishing, 1999), p. 70.

8 See Ernest Becker, *Denial of Death*, (Free Press, 1974), p. 36

9 Hannah Fox is also a professor of theatre and dance at Manhattanville College, located outside of New York City.

10 See *Gathering Voices*, p. 73

11 Christian Penny is currently director of the Toi Whakaara Drama School in Wellington.

12 There are many stories in the press about this issue. For one example, see *The New York Times*, http://nyti.ms/1d0XnFt.

13 Normally, we would first ask the teller to choose an actor to play her own role. However this is a case where the important other is particularly significant.

14 "Fellow-citizens, pardon me, allow me to ask, why am I called upon to speak here to-day? What have I, or those I represent, to do with your national independence? Are the great principles of political freedom and of natural justice, embodied in that Declaration of Independence, extended to us?" Frederick Douglass, "The Meaning of July Fourth for the Negro," July 5, 1852. See http://www.history-isaweapon.com/defcon1/douglassjuly4.html

15 See Barbara Myerhoff, *Number our Days* (Simon & Schuster, 1978), p. 190.

16 See e. e. cummings's *The Enormous Room* (Dover Publications).

17 See "Emerging from Silence: Uschi Sperling Talks to Jonathan Fox," in *Gathering Voices: Essay on Playback Theatre*: http://playbacktheatre.org/wp-content/uploads/2010/04/Uschi.pdf.

18 Barbara Myerhoff, *Stories as Equipment for Living: Last Talks and Tales of Barbara Myerhoff Stories as Equipment for Living* (University of Michigan Press, 2007), p 19.

19 See Esther M. Sternberg, *Healing Spaces: The Science of Place and Well-Being* (Belknap Press, 2010).

20 Paul Woodruff, *Reverence: Renewing a Forgotten Virtue* (Oxford University Press, 2001). My "a sense of your own imperfection" approximates Woodruff's "shame" as a prerequisite for reverence.